THE SOLDIERS

THE SOLDIERS

By the Editors of

TIME-LIFE BOOKS

with text by

David Nevin

TIME-LIFE BOOKS / ALEXANDRIA, VIRGINIA

CONTENTS

1 | Battered cavaliers of the Indian wars

Fear, fatigue, poor rations and little appreciation from his countrymen—that was the lot of the U.S. soldier whose job it was to enforce the nation's arrogant and often muddleheaded Indian policies. In 1845 the territory from the Mississippi to the Pacific Coast was the home of more than 300,000 proud, possessive Indians. Less than 50 years later, the Army had established complete control over the West, and not a single truly free Indian was left.

The common soldier did not necessarily approve of all that happened during those bloody decades. But generally he got the job done, despite appalling odds: in 1867 at the celebrated Wagon Box fight, fewer than 40 soldiers stood off 1,000 warriors. On another occasion, when an officer was asked why his troop had not set up a stronger line of defense, he snapped, "I have no troop, only three men."

Sometimes, as they rested between campaigns, the soldiers found they actually enjoyed the easy camaraderie of the Western outposts. But more often they were out on the Plains making, as the men phrased it, "forty miles a day on beans and hay," praying they would never see an Indian, yet half-wishing that they would find the enemy, have it out once and for all, and go back home.

A U.S. Army officer chivvies a line of soldiers across the Dakota prairie in pursuit of the Sioux.

Looking spruce after a short march out of Fort Davis, Texas, a company of the 3rd Cavalry spreads out on a hillside behind its young officer and his white charger while the noontime coffee water heats over the campfire. The blur in the foreground was caused by a guidon waving in the breeze.

9

Luxuriating in the privilege of rank, two officers of B Company, 7th Infantry, study campaign maps in the shade of a breezeway formed by joining the flies of their tents. While each officer enjoyed his own private shelter, enlisted men slept two or more to a tent — or sometimes in no tent at all.

11

Three cavalrymen warm their hands—and a pot of water—by a Sibley stove in their tent near the end of the Sioux wars. By this late stage of the Indian-fighting, soldiers were equipped with such added luxuries for winter campaigning as the fur hats and arctic overshoes worn by these men.

14

At Camp Pilot Butte in Wyoming, two infantry officers sit beside a staff officer and a bonneted youngster. Enlisted men as well as officers frequently brought their families to posts that had room, but they could be evicted by anyone of a higher rank in a maneuver known as "ranking out."

15

Lined up at evening for the lowering of the flag, privates stand at parade rest in front of their sergeant. These smooth-faced recruits are typical of the youngsters who enlisted for Western adventure, but found tough discipline, extremes of climate and the constant threat of ambush.

16

17

"A bookkeeper, a farm boy, a dentist, a blacksmith"

At about 4 o'clock on the afternoon of September 16, 1868, a party of 50 men led by Major George A. Forsyth rode through a ravine and into the flood plain of the Arikaree River in what now is eastern Colorado. They were all picked hands, wise to the frontier, traveling light on forced march from Fort Wallace, Kansas. Each carried his own gear —a blanket, a canteen, rations for seven days, a Spencer repeating rifle with 140 rounds of ammunition and a Colt's Army revolver with 30 rounds. Four pack mules bore the company's medical supplies and 4,000 supplementary rounds of ammunition for the rifles.

Forsyth was a young man with thick brown hair and a round, boyish face that belied his aggressive nature. He had enlisted in a Chicago regiment of dragoons in 1861 and had risen from private to brevet brigadier general during the Civil War to become the trusted aide of the Union cavalry hero General Philip Sheridan. Now Sheridan, his old commanding officer, was on the frontier as commander of the largest enclave of a vast administrative unit designated as the Division of the Missouri. And George Forsyth, reduced to the permanent rank of major as the Army shrank rapidly after the war, was still functioning as his aide.

Their job was anything but a sinecure. Indian warriors had been striking all over the Great Plains that

In the latter half of the 19th Century the U.S. Army and the Western Indian tribes battled over the land. Each side had its motives, its heroes, its victories and defeats. Recent books have described their confrontations—Sand Creek, the Fetterman fight, Washita, Little Bighorn—from the standpoint of the Indians. This volume tells the story from the soldiers' point of view.

THE EDITORS

year. War parties, many of them Sioux and Cheyenne, had burned settlements, wagon trains, ranches, stage stations, telegraph stations. Sheridan wanted to retaliate. Like every Western soldier blooded in the Civil War's great battles, the general was angered and frustrated by the guerrilla tactics of the Plains Indians. Superb horsemen, they struck where they chose and then drifted away across the Plains with lookouts posted over their back trails. If pursuit came they broke into smaller parties, moving onto stony ground where they left no tracks. Cavalrymen frequently rode their horses to death in the hopeless chase.

Forsyth had offered a solution, proposing to assemble a small force of selected men who could travel light and fast, hunt out the Indians and force them to fight. Sheridan had given his consent to this plan, and now Forsyth and his men, 10 days out of the post, were about to make contact with the enemy. They had been following an Indian trail so heavily beaten it was clear that several villages were on the move ahead. Awed at the apparent number of the enemy, a scout had suggested that Forsyth turn back. "Enlisted to fight Indians, didn't you?" the young leader snapped, and the column rode on. Later that afternoon they turned off the trail and halted in the valley of the Arikaree River.

The valley floor was broad, with rich, high grass. The riverbed was about 140 yards wide but sandy and almost dry at that time of year. A shallow stream coursed through its center, parting to pass a small island perhaps 60 yards long by 20 wide covered with scrubby alder, willow, wild plum and a single cottonwood.

Twelve miles upriver the Indian encampment—made up largely of Sioux but also including a number of Chey-

In the Frederic Remington engraving at left, an officer and a fellow trooper rescue a wounded 10th Cavalryman from Apache bullets. The 10th was one of four black regiments that fought in the Indian wars.

19

left which we intend to eat. on the 4th of July. The flood which is over the bottoms this Spring have killed all the wild strawberries with which it is usually covered; There is no other fruits in this country but plums cherries & service cherries. They say that the cherries are not like our cherries but are like the old fasiond black hearts in Ohio. I have two guns and two dogs and another one I can call mine if I want to & when the sage hens get through breeding I will have some fun and I will have more when the streams get lower and I can fish for trout. I have a short enfield on which I had the sights altered so that you can shoot as close as any hunting rifle Here is the kind of a house we live in

We my fathers square tent with the fly to sit under as a porch in hot weather and a sibley tent which generaly accomadates 17 men below. In the sibley tent we eat & Mr Palidey sleep. Major Bridger & my father sleep in the little lodge as the Major calls it & our cook

ennes and Arapahos — was in turmoil, for a group of Sioux warriors had just galloped into the middle of the village to announce that the soldiers were approaching. As Forsyth had anticipated, however, his force was small enough to entice the more numerous Indians into battle. The warriors collected their fighting ponies and began dressing and painting themselves for war. Among them was one of the greatest of all Indian fighting men. Known as Bat to the other Indians, he was a Cheyenne, large and muscular, with a broad, handsome face dominated by a distinctive hooked nose. To the whites he was known as Roman Nose and his commanding presence in the villages, and Forsyth's on the soldiers' side, ensured that what might have been a skirmish would instead become a deadly battle.

Thinking that they had not yet been detected, Forsyth's men made camp. But the Indians were already moving toward them, scouts ranging ahead to find the soldiers' exact location. At dawn the next day, the warriors were poised on the bluffs overlooking the camp, ready to attack. They numbered about 600, and in the typically individualistic style of the Plains warriors they were disorganized and undisciplined. The engagement began when eight overeager young Indians made an ineffectual attempt to stampede the Army horses. The warriors' war cries alerted Forsyth, and pickets managed to turn back the impulsive attack while the main body of soldiers hastily saddled their mounts.

The enemy seemed everywhere. Scanning the fighting ground, Forsyth perceived that the ravine through which they had entered the valley was not yet closed off, and he scented a trap. From the other direction he saw the first charge — dozens of mounted warriors coming down the dry riverbed on the gallop. Again pickets drove off the attackers, while Forsyth ordered his men to break for the small island that lay just across the river shallows. They made it, and as they brought their horses into a circle and tied them to bushes, forming a living barricade, one of the men cried, "Don't let's stay here and be shot down like dogs!" Forsyth drew his pistol and declared that he would kill any man who tried to leave. Years later, Indians who were there said the move to the island saved Forsyth; they had expected to run down the soldiers one by one on open ground.

As the men tried frantically to dig rifle pits in the sand using tin plates and hunting knives, Forsyth sent three marksmen squirming through the tall grass toward the point of the island that faced the charge. By this time the Indian horde was very close. Lightly armed, firing as they charged, they intended to ride over the island and destroy the soldiers at close quarters. Forsyth remained standing. He moved calmly among his men, surveying their positions and encouraging them until the men themselves insisted that he take cover. When at last the charge hit the point of the island, the soldiers opened such heavy fire from their repeating Spencers that at the last moment the wall of horsemen broke in the center, parted and surged down both sides of the island and beyond it.

The Indians wheeled and, after riding around the island firing at the soldiers, regrouped and charged again. Again the repeating rifle fire broke them, this time at a greater distance. Though Forsyth and several others were hit in those first violent assaults, the fight was just beginning. Many of the Indians were still upriver, waiting as their horses milled nervously. As Forsyth was to learn later, the renowned warrior Roman Nose had not yet entered the fight — for a strange reason: Roman Nose was convinced that he would die if he fought that day. The great Cheyenne believed that he possessed a magical invulnerability to the arrows and bullets of his enemies, and in fact he had often ridden casually through heavy fire without being hit. This supposed invulnerability was thought to stem from a sacred bonnet he wore into battle, and the bonnet's power, in turn, was dependent on the observance of an elaborate set of taboos. But by chance, as Forsyth's men were approaching, Roman Nose had violated one of the taboos and there had been no time for the elaborate purification rites necessary to restore the bonnet's power. As a result, he had held back from the battle. However, when an Indian with the singularly appropriate name of White Contrary accused him of cowardice, he elected to lead the next charge.

His appearance on his great chestnut war pony had a galvanic effect on the other warriors. It unified them in a way rare among Indians in combat. With Roman Nose in the fore, they galloped in a boiling mass down on the little island where Forsyth's men huddled in their shallow rifle pits. The young officer ordered his men to stop firing and reload, six in the magazine, one in the chamber, and hold for orders. They would fire by volleys, and none of them would have time to reload.

Forsyth saw the huge warrior in the lead. Later he remembered that the man was shaking a heavy rifle effortlessly over his head with one hand. The major waited until the rumbling wave of horsemen was a bare 50 yards away and then, grunting with pain, lifted himself and shouted, "Now!"

The volley crashed like cannon fire, and bullets cut down men and horses. But the wave of warriors was not even faintly slowed. The second and third and fourth volleys felled more riders and horses. Those behind leaped over them. The fifth volley staggered the charge, and Forsyth remembered that Roman Nose turned on the chestnut and rallied his men. By the sixth volley Roman Nose was over the position at which the hidden marksmen lay. One of them fired point blank; the ball struck Roman Nose in the back just above his hips and ranged up through his body. The impact of the shot knocked both Roman Nose and his horse down in the shallow water. When his warriors saw their great leader fall, mortally wounded by the shot, the charge faltered and passed by.

On the island, Forsyth turned to the chief scout. "Can they do better than that?" he asked. The man shook his head. In all his years on the Plains, it was the most violent charge he had ever seen. Forsyth's second-in-command, Lieutenant Frederick Beecher, for whom the island eventually was named, lurched toward the major. "I have my death wound, general," the young man said, then collapsed. "Good night," he whispered as he died. The surgeon was dying, too, with a bullet in his forehead. Five others were dead or mortally wounded, and 16 more had been hit. Forsyth had been struck three times: he had taken a glancing shot on the head, his left shin was shattered, and a ball in his right thigh was lodged against the femoral artery.

The Indians continued to charge sporadically, and riflemen on the surrounding bluffs held Forsyth's men under siege for more than a week. The wounded soldiers suffered terribly; Forsyth's thigh wound was extremely painful, and on the fourth day of the siege, he asked his men to cut the bullet out. They refused, fearful that a slip of the knife would nick the artery and kill him. Forsyth asked for his saddlebags, took out his razor, told two men to hold open the wound and, with nothing to deaden the pain, carefully carved his own

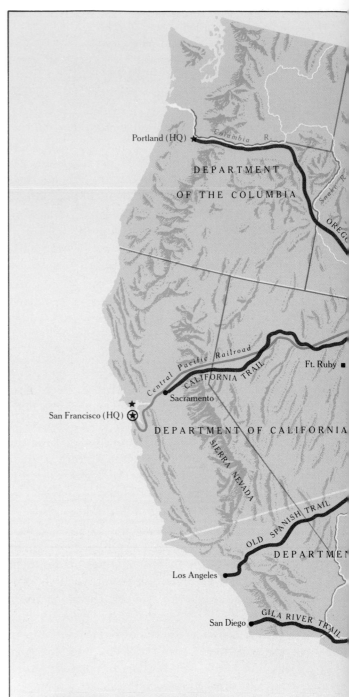

A SOLDIER'S MAP OF THE OLD WEST
During the decisive years of the Indian wars, from 1865 to 1876, the Army's troops were strung out in isolated forts (the major ones are shown here) across the 2.5 million square miles from the Mississippi to the Pacific. Rarely more than 15,000 men, they had a mission that seemed impossible: to protect trails; to defend miners, settlers and cattlemen; to survey railroad lines and guard construction crews; to engage the enemy in battles of extermination like those indicated on this map. But they managed, winning more often than they lost—and in the end, they secured the West for white settlement.

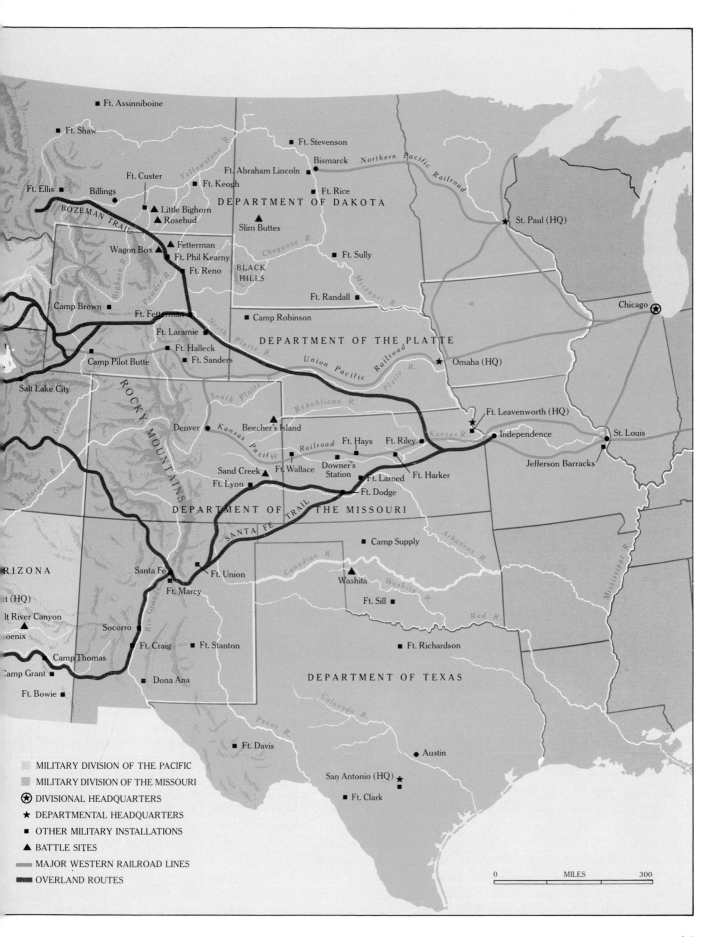

Ft. Assinniboine

Ft. Shaw

Ft. Ellis
Billings
Ft. Custer
Ft. Keogh

Ft. Stevenson

Bismarck
Ft. Abraham Lincoln

Northern Pacific Railroad

Ft. Rice

DEPARTMENT OF DAKOTA

BOZEMAN TRAIL

Little Bighorn
Rosebud

Slim Buttes

Fetterman
Wagon Box
Ft. Phil Kearny
Ft. Reno

Camp Brown

Ft. Fetterman

Ft. Laramie

Ft. Halleck
Camp Pilot Butte
Ft. Sanders

Yellowstone R.

Bighorn R.

Powder R.

Cheyenne R.

BLACK
HILLS

Ft. Sully

Missouri R.

Ft. Randall

Camp Robinson

DEPARTMENT OF THE PLATTE

St. Paul (HQ)

Chicago

Ft. Leavenworth (HQ)

North Platte R.

Union Pacific Railroad

Platte R.

Omaha (HQ)

ROCKY MOUNTAINS

Salt Lake City

Green R.

Colorado R.

South Platte R.

Denver

Beecher's Island

Republican R.

Kansas Pacific *Railroad*

Ft. Hays
Ft. Riley

Independence

Kansas R.

St. Louis

Jefferson Barracks

Sand Creek
Ft. Wallace
Ft. Lyon

Downer's
Station

Ft. Larned
Ft. Dodge

Ft. Harker

DEPARTMENT OF THE MISSOURI

SANTA FE TRAIL

Camp Supply

Arkansas R.

RIZONA

t (HQ)
lt River Canyon
oenix

Camp Thomas
Camp Grant

Ft. Bowie

Santa Fe
Ft. Marcy

Socorro

Ft. Craig

Dona Ana

Ft. Union

Rio Grande

Ft. Stanton

Washita

Ft. Sill

Canadian R.

Washita R.

Red R.

Ft. Richardson

DEPARTMENT OF TEXAS

Pecos R.

Ft. Davis

Colorado R.

Austin

San Antonio (HQ)

Ft. Clark

Mississippi R.

MILITARY DIVISION OF THE PACIFIC
MILITARY DIVISION OF THE MISSOURI
DIVISIONAL HEADQUARTERS
DEPARTMENTAL HEADQUARTERS
OTHER MILITARY INSTALLATIONS
BATTLE SITES
MAJOR WESTERN RAILROAD LINES
OVERLAND ROUTES

0   MILES   300

23

A portrait of Indian-fighter George Forsyth projects the mettle he later showed under siege at Beecher's Island, Colorado. A relief force arrived to find the wounded major coolly reading the novel *Oliver Twist*.

flesh until the bullet dropped free.

Meanwhile two pairs of scouts had slipped away from the island to try to get help. The first pair left the night after Roman Nose's attack, sneaking through the Indian lines and walking backward so their tracks would look like those of Indian moccasins heading toward the island. Once in the clear, they made for Fort Wallace 110 miles distant, walking by night and hiding by day. Two days later Forsyth dispatched the second pair. Somehow all four men managed to elude the Indians and alert a relief force. When the fresh column of troops arrived at the island, Forsyth's men had been reduced to eating the putrid meat of horses that had been killed in the fighting.

The story of Forsyth, standing fast on Beecher's Island as the savage warriors thundered down upon him, was told and retold in barracks and around campfires all across the Plains. Accounts of it filled the press and the popular histories of the time. The fight itself was not strategically significant; yet the Battle of Beecher's Island remained one of the most celebrated in the annals of the Plains. In Forsyth, soldiers all over the West saw their own self-image as Indian fighters: outnumbered and surrounded, but steadfast under fire, heroic under prolonged siege. And although only nine Indians had died that day at Beecher's Island, Forsyth's men did not know it; they boasted of having slain hundreds — and soldiers everywhere were proud.

The fact is that U.S. soldiers on Western duty had little enough to cheer about. They were poor, hardy and long-suffering men. Few had been fully trained, and many were neither good horsemen nor good riflemen. They were not skilled at living off the country as were the Indians, nor were they fitted to the guerrilla tactics that were merely an extension of the Indian's hunting skills. Their pay was miserly — only $16 a month for a private when the Civil War ended, reduced to $13 by a parsimonious Congress during an economy wave in 1871. Few of the men ever saw even that pittance, for they were constantly in debt to the various sergeants and storekeepers who functioned informally as bankers and loan sharks on the frontier outposts.

The soldiers' food was about on a level with their pay; and their service was arduous and thankless. It is a tribute to their nature that they remained generally in good spirits and, with rare exceptions, actually did bravely face an enemy that usually outnumbered them when the fight finally came.

In all, the years from 1865 to 1876 when Indian warfare built toward its climax were not a happy time for the Army. After the Civil War more than a million volunteers were mustered out in a year, and the Army was reduced to a small core of regulars. Generals shrank to colonels and colonels to lieutenants. When Forsyth stood pistol in hand to stop the men who threatened to quit Beecher's Island, the man who backed him with rifle ready was his first sergeant, William H. H. McCall. McCall was a particularly authoritative sergeant, for during the Civil War he had been brevetted a brigadier general and had commanded a Pennsylvania regiment.

The country's interest in the Army had sunk to zero. People were tired of war, and the problems of the West seemed as unreal as they were remote. After one terrible conflict on the nation's own ground, people were not ready for another. It was coming, nonetheless. The country had embarked on a collision course with the Plains Indians. Within a few years that great issue would be decided by the handful of soldiers who manned the lonely, dusty posts of the West.

The men on these posts were members of the regular Army, all volunteers, signed up for three- and five-year hitches. They came from virtually all levels of American society. In his memoirs, Forsyth noted that his troops on one expedition included "a bookkeeper, a farm boy, a dentist and a blacksmith, a young man of position trying to gain a commission and a salesman ruined by drink, an ivory carver and a Bowery tough" —all in a wagon-train escort one morning in 1865.

For recruits there were few requirements beyond reasonable health. Some enlistees were immigrants barely able to speak English. Some had served in foreign armies and saw the U.S. Army as a likely place to learn the new country's ways in familiar circumstances. The Irish soldier, like the Irish policeman, was so common as to be a stock character. Youngsters joined in hope of learning to read and write and cipher—some regiments actually held classes. Boys caught up in the romance of the West saw the Army as a place to act out a glamorous role. A fair number joined for plain economic reasons—jobs were hard to come by in the postwar slump. Others wanted to see the country, to escape a woman, to avoid trouble they saw drifting close, to shake the bottle, to escape the drudgery of the family farm. Some were criminals avoiding capture, and many enlisted under false names. A few were chronic deserters, reentering under one name after another until an exasperated general proposed tattooing miscreants to avoid reenlisting any "drunkards, obscene fellows, worthless men and deserters." Among the steadiest and most reliable soldiers were those in four black regiments, recruited by a Congressional act of 1866 and sent to fight on the Plains. They fought frequently and hard, deserting far less often than whites and holding onto both discipline and morale during winter marches when white soldiers faltered. Yet they remained cordoned off in their own units, segregated from the rest of the Army, and when they went into action field dispatches mentioned them as having been merely "engaged." White officers shunned duty with the black regiments, regarding it as a form of exile. (In a letter home one young blade rationalized his stay with a black regiment by noting, "I won't have near as much to do with them personally as you would with a black cook.") To the Indians, however, the blacks were respected antagonists whom the warriors called "the Buffalo Soldiers." The term came from a resemblance Indians saw between the black soldier's hair and the buffalo's shaggy coat; and according to some scholars, since the buffalo was a sacred animal,

the Indians honored the blacks by linking them with it.

Officers of the West were just as diverse a group as the men who served under them—although not a single black man served as an officer in the Indian wars. Some were vicious drivers. George Armstrong Custer was known to an adoring nation as the gallant boy-general, but his men called him "Hard Ass" and many hated him for the brutal and often pointless forced marches he imposed on them. Some, like General Nelson Miles, who eventually clawed his way up to Commander in Chief of the Army, were intensely ambitious; others were content to make captain through a hard lifetime in the saddle. Some officers carried volumes of the classics in the original Latin and Greek in their saddlebags. Others were barely literate, and many were alcoholics. But all officers were conscious of their caste.

Officers held themselves totally apart from enlisted men, except on campaigns when shared hazards tended to promote some degree of camaraderie. On the posts, officers spoke to sergeants and the sergeants, in turn, spoke to the lower ranks. The social difference was so vast that posts big enough to have schools maintained two, so that the children of officers and enlisted men need not mingle. The better officers, who bothered to interest themselves in their men's diet and welfare, expressed their concern in a spirit of *noblesse oblige* that was without personal overtones.

Despite such prejudice and the neglect that frequently went with it, soldiers on balance managed to behave as good and decent men. In their comments, their diaries and letters, their actions and reactions, there is a solidity and an engaging simplicity. Although many deserted, the majority made the best of a bad lot. As a group they were physically tough, usually ignorant, their pleasures simple, their attitudes straightforward. Like all soldiers in all wars they griped, but for the most part they also accepted their lonely, perilous lot.

The posts they manned often were hundreds of miles from the nearest railhead. The soldiers reached these remote stations on foot or on horseback, marching in long columns under constant danger of Indian raids. One recruit remembered the joy his whole party felt on a day in 1866 when they realized that Indians on the horizon were merely chasing buffalo. The same recruit encountered an ox strayed from some caravan of settlers. "May I shoot it?" he asked his officer hungrily. "Sure-

A painting by Robert Lindneux depicts the wounded Major George Forsyth (*center, holding pistol*) and his besieged command on Beecher's Island, Colorado, awaiting the climactic charge of Cheyenne warriors. Their leader, Roman Nose, was felled by a bullet, and the Indians withdrew.

ly," came the answer. "We need fresh meat and the Indians will get the stray if we don't."

The toughest, most ferocious Indians in North America lived in the West, as part of a total Indian population of 200,000 between the Mississippi and the eastern slopes of the Sierras. But the U.S. Army, after 1870, rarely embraced more than 25,000 men. Only a small portion of these — at one point in 1868 the total was no more than 2,600 — went to the posts scattered across the hostile immensity. Some outposts had fewer than 50 men and many had a mere three companies, perhaps 200 or 300 men in all.

Not all the stations were permanent establishments. The frontier was in flux, and the Army, moving with the line of settlement, rapidly established new forts and sometimes just as rapidly abandoned them. Thus when a footsore column arrived at its assigned station, the men often had to build their own post. Tents went up and the weary work of construction began. In the Southwest, the post structures were made of adobe — chunks of claylike sod laboriously hacked from the earth. After these crude, dirty bricks had dried in the sun they were stacked up to form walls. Naturally, the soldiers did the work themselves, and hated it.

In the North, some buildings were of adobe, still others were built of logs or split boards. In the latter case, once a site had been selected and camp pitched, everyone except the guard mount marched to the nearest available timber, which might be miles away. There the men felled trees, trimmed them into logs and hauled

Early Western campaigns: The Mexican War

A generation before the Indian wars, the U.S. Army embarked on its first major venture west of the Mississippi.

It began as a brazen bit of saber rattling by President Polk, who sent 10 regiments to the Rio Grande in 1846 in an attempt to force Mexico to sell California and the Southwest to the United States. Since the Rio Grande was in disputed territory, Mexico regarded the act as an invasion, and war quickly broke out — notwithstanding "all our efforts to avoid it," as Polk self-righteously claimed.

In the initial clash of armies in early May, 1846, General Zachary Taylor's 2,000 regulars, although outnumbered, routed the overconfident Mexicans by superior marksmanship and expert use of artillery.

Facing total forces of more than 30,000 men, Taylor could not drive into Mexico without reinforcements. But volunteers proved easy to come by: within a few months 50,000 recruits had signed up for glory and adventure in the Halls of Montezuma. Raw but eager, these "wild volunteers," as General Taylor called them, massed in Texas, where they soon grew impatient with drills in the blazing summer sun and spent much of their time drinking, brawling and earning the contempt of the regulars.

But when Taylor thrust into Mexico, the new soldiers fought ferociously. The fortified city of Monterrey (right) fell on September 25 at a cost of almost 500 casualties. Taylor ended his campaign with a narrow victory at Buena Vista — won when a cavalry charge broke the surrounding Mexican lines. The charge was led by a colonel named Jefferson Davis, whose comrades in arms included such other young West Point graduates as Robert E. Lee, Ulysses S. Grant and George McClellan.

While Taylor bludgeoned his way southward General Stephen Kearny's Army of the West marched from the Missouri to California. He did not encounter significant resistance until he approached San Diego, and within a month the province was secured. In the main theater of the war, the crushing blow was delivered by General Winfield Scott, who attacked inland from Veracruz and on September 14, 1847, captured Mexico City.

The swift victory over Mexico heaped glory on the Army, and two of its generals — Zachary Taylor and Franklin Pierce, who served under Scott — would become Presidents in the next decade. But it cost 13,000 American lives, the great majority of them lost to diseases such as dysentery and smallpox. And after the war the Army had the additional burden of protecting the half-million square miles of territory it had won. The Indian tribes of the area — Navaho, Apache and Ute — would keep U.S. soldiers busy there for 40 more years.

them back. Floors were usually of earth and so were roof coverings. Fort Stevenson in Dakota was erected in winter with warmed mud — which quickly froze again. When stoves were lighted inside, spatters of remelted mud fell from the ceiling all winter long.

When she was traveling overland into Dakota Territory, Custer's wife Elizabeth saw a post manned by 50 infantrymen and observed that "the soldiers' barracks, officers' quarters, and storehouses were huddled together inside a wall made of logs. The sand was so deep about this spot that nothing could be made to grow. Constant gusts of wind over the unprotected plain kept little clouds of fine alkaline dust whirling in the air and filling the eyes and mouth; not a tree was near. The frail buildings rocked and swayed. No one could

go outside to ride or hunt without peril." The peril was, of course, from Indians. Earlier, when Mrs. Custer had twitted a handsome young officer because he was still a bachelor, he had said she would understand when she passed his station. She did.

These hastily built forts, thrown up in the middle of nowhere, stood as the advance guard for a moving tide of civilization that, in the years right after the Civil War, quickly engulfed the trans-Mississippi wilderness. Thanks to reports from earlier explorers, miners and emigrants, the old idea that the Plains comprised an uninhabitable desert, suitable only for aborigines and buffalo, was fading away. Miners had already exhausted the surface lodes in the mountains and were streaming into the foothills from the west in search of the last gold

Charging through cannon fire, Zachary Taylor's troops fight their way up the steps of the Bishop's Palace in Monterrey, Mexico.

that could still be gathered by an individual with a pan. Behind them came restless settlers and displaced Southerners looking for a new life. In the sinewy Texas longhorn, cattlemen found a creature that could endure the harsh climate of the Plains, and new equipment such as steel plows made it possible to farm the prairie. The wagon trails were busy, and iron rails reached east and west toward a meeting in Utah.

In such expansive times little thought was given to the fact that the coveted land was already occupied. The trouble that was brewing, that simply had to come when the white man and red man met, was made the worse by the quickness with which it all happened. In 1878 William Tecumseh Sherman, then Commanding General of the Army, wrote in amazement that "this vast region has undergone in the past ten years a more violent and radical change than any like space of the earth's surface during any previous fifty years."

The soldiers were caught in the middle, bound by duty to enforce the white man's claim to the land, yet unable by their own situations to profit from it. Each of the new people who came — the miner, rancher, farmer, townsman in fresh-sprung hamlets, freighter, rail layer — looked to the soldier to save himself and his family and property from the fury of the Plains Indians, whose livelihood was being snatched away.

The Indians' anger took the form of attacks on isolated ranches, on stage stations, on wagon trains that carried too few riflemen, on railroad gangs cut off from the main bodies of builders. After each desperate en-

Early Western campaigns: The Mormon challenge

Nine years after the Mexican War ended, the Army sent another large force west, this time against a most unlikely enemy: the Church of Jesus Christ of Latter-day Saints, better known as the Mormons.

During the late 1840s, persecuted and abhorred for their practice of polygamy, the Mormons fled into the wilderness and established the center of a new civilization in the Valley of Great Salt Lake. Through cooperative enterprise and extensive irrigation, they won a handsome living from the arid soil of the region.

Within a decade, the frontier had caught up with them. Now, however, as prior occupants of the land, the Mormons held the strings of power, and they made the most of their advantage. When Utah was made a territory in 1850, their leader, Brigham Young, was named governor. Resisting federal authority at every turn, he administered the territory as a Mor-

mon kingdom. Most unforgivable of all, he undeniably had 27 wives.

Soon after President James Buchanan assumed office in 1857, he decided to replace Young with a non-Mormon governor, Alfred Cumming, a grossly fat former Indian agent. And when the Mormons made it clear that they intended to prevent Cumming from assuming office, the President ordered the Army out. In mid-July, a force of 2,500 soldiers began its departure from Fort Leavenworth, Kansas, headed toward Utah to back up Cumming with guns. The march west, covering 1,200 miles and lasting almost four months, became a horror when winter overtook the troops (right). Worse, Brigham Young, describing the U.S. government as "a stink in our nostrils," directed his Mormon militia to harass the advancing column by laying waste the countryside, blockading roads and even destroying government supply trains.

These guerrilla tactics were so successful that when the force reached the vicinity of Salt Lake in November it was exhausted.

Not until spring, when fresh supplies and new horses and mules arrived, was the Army in a position to meet the Mormon challenge. But by then a compromise had been arranged. Cumming would enter Salt Lake City and be accepted as governor, but the Army would remain behind. Satisfied with this arrangement, President Buchanan pardoned all insurgents. As tempers cooled, Young agreed to let the Army save face by marching into Salt Lake City — and straight out the other side again.

So, in a magnificent anticlimax and without a shot being fired, the Mormon War came to an end. However, one basic conflict — the practice of polygamy so abhorred by Easterners — remained unsolved. It was finally outlawed by a federal act in 1882.

counter, tattered survivors hastened to the nearest Army post to demand help. The bugle sounded and the men leaped to horse and rode off in a pursuit that usually became a grinding, hungry, thirsty, exhausting ordeal. The trail might peter out with no Indians even sighted, or it might end in a sudden battle, begun from ambush and soon finished, with soldiers wounded and dying while the enemy vanished once more.

Civilians were not at all shy about calling on the Army for help. Let a man lose so much as a cow and he was at the nearest post insisting that all the Indians from here to there be wiped out in retaliation. Many a disgusted cavalry troop marched for hours seeking Indian cow thieves only to find that the cows had merely strayed. Then, often enough, the soldiers found that the settler expected them to pay well for the rations the famished troops bought from his farm.

As the railroads began to push out beyond the frontier, soldiers could ride part of the way toward combat. But most of their marches were still made the hard way, by infantrymen on foot and by cavalrymen mounted on horses that had to be curried and tended and watched over morning and night. Some of these marches lasted for weeks, covering hundreds of miles. When the men came back, they had long hair, ragged beards and torn clothing. Often the soldiers went out in the face of blizzards with the wind howling and the temperature below zero: officers sometimes had to whip the men to keep them awake and thus alive. At other times the route of march lay through deserts where the tem-

A blizzard engulfs an Army column sent against the Mormons in 1857. The loss of horses and mules nearly wrecked the expedition.

perature soared to 120° in the daytime, and the men staggered from water hole to water hole, all too frequently coming to dry holes. Every canyon, every copse was a potential trap; every mountain, every mesa was a watching post for nimble Indian scouts. Rarely could soldiers move without their progress being reported, often with puffs of smoke mounting in a still sky.

The country was new and strange to these recruits. And their officers were still geared to the tactics and practices of the Civil War, which had been fought over wooded, rich terrain in set-piece battles totally different from the guerrilla clashes of the Indian wars. But the Army as an institution was not new to the West.

Much of the early trans-Mississippi exploration had been led by Army officers—Lewis and Clark, Zebulon Pike, John Charles Frémont and others. As early as 1835 Colonel Henry Dodge took a party of dragoons along the Oregon Trail as a demonstration of power designed to impress the Indians. And a decade later the veteran frontier officer, Colonel Stephen Kearny, led five companies of the 1st Dragoons on a vast circular patrol through the Rocky Mountains, also aimed at awing the Indians. In 1846 large numbers of troops marched into the Southwest on their way to the Mexican War—through which the United States ultimately acquired a huge tract of land stretching from Texas to California. During 1857 and 1858 other Army troops slogged the bitter miles from Kansas to Utah, and to New Mexico and back in a campaign to subdue stubborn and unruly Mormons. And while the Civil War was under way, the famed scout Colonel Kit Carson guided a force that killed or captured some 9,000 Navajo, permanently breaking the power of that tribe.

After the war the Army's role in the West changed radically, as did the West itself when the surge of settlers plunged into country that once had been free to the buffalo and the wild hunter. While the Army shrank in size, the territory it was required to cover expanded. The Indians, forced off their home grounds onto the bleak High Plains and into the mountains, were coming to realize that there was no refuge. Now they were fighting not just for ground or pride or custom but for survival. And for the 10 years from 1866 to 1876 they engaged the Army in no less than 200 fights.

Thus the soldiers in the field faced an increasingly determined enemy at a time when their own government vacillated between wishing the problem would go away and deciding it was not that serious after all. This vacillation was the real reason that soldiers of the time were undèrequipped, underfed and underpaid. For one absurd five-month period in 1877, while Congress fumed and faddled about economy, the Army got no pay at all. The truth was the United States government simply could not get itself together and face the fact that it had a genuine crisis on its hands.

The soldiers' task was made doubly difficult by the graft that ran through the government's dealings with Indians. Soldiers knew that Indians were forever being cheated of the rations promised to them in return for surrender of this or that piece of hunting ground. Often they felt sympathy for the victims of such dubious dealing. And they were galled by the knowledge that this cheating, which enriched thieving Western traders and political hacks in the East, sooner or later led to fighting in which the lowly private risked his life.

Another sore point with the soldiers stemmed from the government's decision to manage Indian affairs—short of combat—through the civilian Indian Bureau, under the Department of the Interior. The bureau was trying to placate the tribes by giving good weapons and ammunition to Indians who were not openly hostile. The purpose of arming the tribes was to increase their hunting capacities; supposedly this would make up for the reduction of their hunting grounds by white settlement. But since most Indians tended to vary between hostility to and friendly dependence on whites, soldiers sometimes found themselves the targets of the new hunting weapons.

Paradoxically, the Army had been delegated the job of enforcing treaties designed to protect Indian land from white penetration. But even if senior officers agreed with the wisdom of such treaties—which they didn't—they would not have had enough troops to seal off reservations from the oncoming swarms of settlers.

And so both Indians and soldiers blundered toward the final bloodletting. The Indians had no real chance, of course. That much was clear to the generals who sent troops against them. The Plains Tribes were helpless in the long run against a highly organized enemy. Furthermore, since the warrior bands had no industrial base, they could not sustain a fight. Hence they could

The fighting song of Custer's 7th Cavalry — played as the men charged at Washita *(pages 34-35)* and later at Little Bighorn — was an Irish drinking ballad that honored the bold men of the town of Garryowen.

not hold what they had won. Most battles ended with the Indians in retreat — whether or not they had lost — because their supplies were exhausted.

The Indians were, in fact, essentially a stone-age people, recently introduced to the technology and social structure of the whites but having neither the capacity nor the desire to reproduce either one. Their own concept of society was as a diffused collection of tribal groups acting autonomously. They saw life itself as controlled by numerous spirits, and they sensed no god-mandate to improve themselves or to conquer the wilderness about them.

Unlike the powerful, exploitative white people now crushing in from every side, the Plains Indians did not develop the land at all in the sense of increasing and channeling its productivity. With very minor excep-

tions, they raised virtually nothing themselves, but merely used what grew naturally — wild fruits and wild animals, most importantly the buffalo. Its skin provided their robes, shelter and even their boats, its meat their food, its sinews many of their tools, its chips their fuel. The Indians considered the unplowed, unfenced buffalo country to be well and properly used. But the white men came to the Plains with a several-thousand-year tradition of working soil in carefully measured and clearly owned plots. Naturally they could not accept the idea that a huge tract of land merely hunted over was being properly utilized.

In this tragic culture clash, neither side seemed interested in understanding the attitudes and thought processes of the other. Each saw the other in racist terms. Both Sherman and Sheridan believed in the innate inferiority of the Indians and in the righteousness of the white advance to the West. Indians, in Sherman's words, were "a class of savages displaced by the irresistible progress of our race." He added that "treachery is inherent in the Indian character."

Indian tribes, for their own part, usually saw themselves as naturally superior not only to all white men but to other Indians as well. Most tribal names meant, in translation, something like "the people."

Such exalted self-images on both sides left little incentive to adapt and learn. All whites resembled one another to the Indians, who held them individually and collectively in contempt. General Sherman offered a mirror-image view when he wrote to President Grant that Indians "all look alike and to get the rascals, we are forced to include all." When whites decided to punish the hostiles, they attacked available Indians; when Indians were angry they attacked the nearest whites. Each considered that his own attacks were justified, whereas the other's were wanton and murderous.

Inevitably the attitudes of the generals filtered down through the ranks and infected the enlisted soldier. He shared the opinion that the westward expansion of white Americans was God-ordained, and he saw himself as the vanguard and the protector of a chosen people. Those who stood in the way were brutal heathens, more or less subhuman. This view was enhanced, of course, by the white soldier's perception of the Indian's mystical culture as nonsensical and contemptible. The attitude that the Indians were no more than savages

Custer's 7th Cavalry slashes through a Cheyenne camp near the Washita River in this painting by Charles Schreyvogel. Although soldiers who fought in the battle praised the accuracy of this depiction, the Indians in fact did not have time to mount their horses when the village was hit.

was permanently frozen for the soldier the first time he found the remains of a comrade who had been mutilated or cooked alive over an open fire.

A few senior officers expressed an abstract sort of sympathy toward the Indians as a people, usually well after the fact. Sheridan wrote: "We took away their country, broke up their mode of living, their habits of life, introduced disease and decay among them, and it was for this and against this that they made war. Could anyone expect less?" But most of the correspondence of officers carried a continuing theme of extermination as the solution to the Indian problem. "I suppose they must be exterminated," General Sherman said of the Sioux and the Cheyennes in a letter to his brother. In 1866 he lectured General Grant, "We must act with vindicative earnestness against the Sioux, even to their extermination, men, women and children." Sherman expected that the railroad would enable him to realize this policy by increasing his mobility against the Indians. As soon as it was completed, he wrote in 1867, "we can act so energetically that both Sioux and Cheyennes must die or submit to our dictation."

Even before the railroad was finished, the Army found a tactic that would effectively destroy the warrior tribes. Devised by General Sheridan, it was called the winter campaign. In the days that followed the fight on Beecher's Island, Sheridan concluded that while Forsyth's foray had been gallant enough, it had not changed the basic military situation. More than ever, he was determined to break the enemy's back. His solution was not to engage war parties in frontal combat but to strike at the Indians' base — their villages, their food supplies and their families.

Essentially nomadic, the Plains Indians were immobilized only during the winter. The rest of the year they were on the move, following the ripening grass and the game. Their wars, which they had conducted among themselves long before the white men came, took place in the summer. In the fall they broke off for the buffalo hunts that produced the food and shelter to see them through the winter when no other food was available. On the Plains, where there was no natural shelter to break the icy wind, winter was deadly. Crusted snow covered the grass, and the ponies grew thin and weak; normally it took several weeks of spring grazing to restore the strength of the Indians' mounts. During this cold season the tribes made semipermanent camps along streams where there was a wood supply and a sheltering bluff, and there they waited for the sun to return.

The way to get at the Indians, Sheridan decided, was to go out in winter, find the villages, kill as many Indians as possible, burn their food and their shelter, kill their horses and drive the survivors out onto the frozen Plains on foot. It would not be easy: when Jim Bridger, the famed frontiersman, first heard the proposal, he said, "You can't hunt Indians on the plains in winter, for blizzards don't respect man or beast." But Sheridan laid his plans. On November 23, 1868, a bare two months after Forsyth's battle, the first winter campaign began. Sheridan's agent for the initial strike was his favorite officer, the vainglorious George Armstrong Custer.

On the dawn of that November day, Lieutenant Colonel Custer readied his 7th Cavalry to ride forth from Camp Supply in what now is western Oklahoma. A blizzard was blowing, and the temperature had dropped below zero. "What do you think?" Sheridan asked Custer, remembering Bridger's remark. "It's all right," Custer said. "We can move. The Indians can't."

Naturally nobody asked the opinion of the 800 soldiers of the 7th Cavalry, wearing long blue overcoats and fur hats and mounted on shivering horses. Obviously, given any choice they would at that moment have been tucked in warm barracks, a roaring fire in the stove, as glad as any Indian not to feel the blood in their feet and fingers gradually forming ice crystals. Moreover, if anyone had polled them on their feelings about making war on women and children, about driving the aged and the newborn naked and hungry across the endless snow, almost certainly they would have found the prospect repulsive. But no one asks soldiers.

When the 7th Cavalry set off, the snow was blowing so thick and hard that even the scouts couldn't see. Custer, who regularly drove his men to their endurance and beyond, led the way with pocket compass in hand, planning to head due south until he picked up signs of Indians. The first night he camped 15 miles from the post. In the cutting wind, it took the men hours to peg down their tents. Then during the night, the snow stopped. The temperature in the morning was -7°. The men saddled and marched.

Four days later they struck the Canadian River, smashed the surface ice and prepared to ford. Custer

Mutilated after his death, a cavalryman's corpse lies on the Kansas prairie in 1867. Indians maimed the bodies of enemies in the belief that the slain men's spirits would then be identically crippled in the afterlife.

sent Major Joel Elliott upriver to scout. By the time the command had crossed the Canadian, a messenger had come from Elliott reporting that he had struck an Indian trail leading south toward the Washita River. Custer gave the rider a new horse and sent him back to Elliott with instructions to follow the trail until 8 p.m., then stop and wait. Custer found Elliott at 9 that night in a draw where small fires were possible. He gave the men an hour in which to brew their coffee and eat some hardtack. The day was Thanksgiving, 1868.

At 10 p.m. the moon rose and the command moved out, with a pair of Osage Indian scouts walking ahead. Presently the Indians stopped. They smelled fire. Custer could smell nothing and believed that his scouts were afraid. But the scouts moved on and soon all saw the embers of a dying fire. Investigating, the scouts concluded that a pony herd had been there and that boys assigned to watch it had lighted the fire for warmth. A village must be near. The troops pushed ahead, pausing

at each hill crest, and presently they saw a village of about 75 lodges lying below on the banks of the Washita River. Smoke from dying fires curled in the still air over some of the tipis. Custer heard a pony bell, signifying a herd. A dog yelped. Clear in the silence, an infant wailed. He divided his command so that at dawn it would attack from all four quarters. Then he ordered his men to wait for daylight. They stood to their arms, the cold seeping into their bodies.

Custer did not know who was in the village or even exactly where he was. He did not reconnoiter. He simply prepared to attack. As it turned out, the village was Cheyenne, led by Chief Black Kettle, survivor of a terrible massacre at Sand Creek in 1864 when volunteers attacked a village that believed itself to be under Army protection. Both before and after the Sand Creek massacre, Black Kettle had accepted the inevitability of the white encroachment and had worked for peace. But Custer's soldiers knew none of these things. They

37

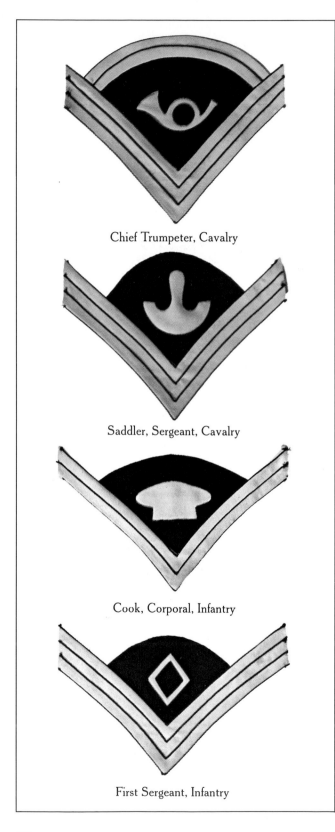

Chief Trumpeter, Cavalry

Saddler, Sergeant, Cavalry

Cook, Corporal, Infantry

First Sergeant, Infantry

were aware only that they were deployed for action.

Fog lay heavy in the Washita River valley that dawn. As the light glimmered in the east, Custer's contingent, including the 7th's band, rode across the bottoms, packs rattling, harnesses jingling, snow muffling the hoof beats. The village ahead remained quiet. Almost all its people were still asleep, wrapped in warm buffalo robes. Then suddenly from the Indian encampment a rifle shot rang out. Custer called for the charge and turned to his bandsmen, crying "Play!" The musicians brought their freezing instruments to their lips and burst forth with the 7th's fighting song, "Garryowen," ragged and weirdly incongruous in that place. Under the bugle notes the 7th attacked from all four sides, galloping among the lodges, shooting at whoever emerged. Many of the Indians leaped naked from their robes, some armed, some simply running, herding their women and children before them. They dashed into the icy river and waded downstream, keeping near the sheltering banks and breaking the ice as they went. Now that the tension of the long frozen night was released, the soldiers rode among the enemy, shooting, slashing, yelling and cursing.

In a few minutes the Indians' feeble resistance was over. Black Kettle and his wife lay dead in the village. Some Indian men, women and children had escaped, but others, all women and children, were captured in the tipis. General Sheridan's orders had specified killing warriors, but it is hard for soldiers to discriminate at such times, and probably most of those killed were women and children. Custer reported that 105 Indians had been killed and 53 women and children captured. His losses in the village attack were six soldiers killed and several wounded. By implication the Indian dead were warriors; but the number of warriors actually killed, according to subsequent reports, was probably no more than 38.

Since Custer had not reconnoitered, he did not realize that Black Kettle's was only the first of several villages strung along the Washita, and that many more Indians than he had expected were on hand. Major Elliott, leading a group of 19 men after fleeing survivors, was later ambushed and killed with all his men. Custer made only a quick search for Elliott; the frozen bodies of the massacred squad were not found until weeks later. And Custer's stunningly callous abandonment of

Elliott's small, outnumbered force after a token search was an act that was to hound Custer the rest of his life.

Before leaving, however, Custer pulled down Black Kettle's lodges and burned them, along with all the village food stores and implements, including clothes. He herded 700 ponies into a draw and slaughtered them. Then, driving his captives before him, he returned to a hero's welcome at Camp Supply with his band once again playing "Garryowen." Sheridan was delighted, and his superior, Sherman, wired congratulations. Black Kettle's people were broken, of course. Naked, starving, their shelter destroyed, the winter stretching before them, those who survived the bullets and the cold eventually crept into the post to surrender. This was a pattern that was repeated again and again all over the western Plains until the Indians' power was permanently destroyed.

The tactics as well as the attitudes of these generals were, beyond question, harsh in the extreme. And the actions of their soldiers were often brutal. During the subsequent years of the Indian wars, there would be other cold-blooded slaughters like that at the Washita, and these were more typical of Indian warfare than was the glorious stand at Beecher's Island. Yet often, especially in the early days, other soldiers would indeed experience the terror of an ambush such as Major Forsyth's fight, or the exhaustion of a long march or the aching fear of a lonely night guard. The soldiers assumed that if they were captured they would be tortured. And they knew for certain that they would be killed, for there were no prisoners of war.

Theirs was a world in which mercy had little place. They fought engagements in which they were usually outnumbered. Sometimes their foe had better weapons, sold by profiteering traders in the frontier posts or given outright to the Indians by the terms of treaties concocted in Washington. Moreover, the Plains warriors were better horsemen and more fanatical fighters than the soldiers; Indian warriors knew the terrain perfectly and could move as silently as the dust.

To the soldiers of the Old West, the measure of the Indian wars would remain the felling of Roman Nose on the sixth volley when the seventh was the last; crouched on the ground and facing the onslaught of 600 horsemen thundering at them. These soldiers, downtrodden yet proud, are the men of our story.

Hospital Steward, Medical

Drum Major, Artillery

Stable Sergeant, Artillery

Commissary Sergeant, Artillery

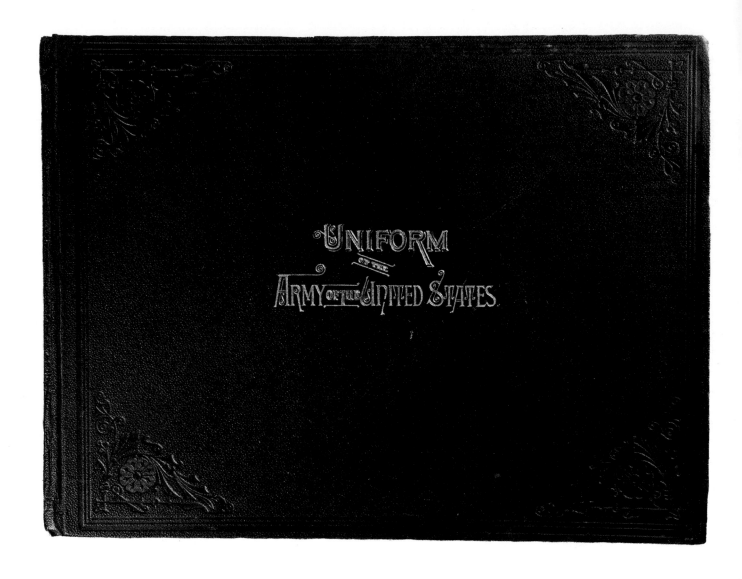

Soldiers on the Western frontier had a grubby, dusty, sweaty job to do, and most of the time they looked it. On ordinary duty days, they slouched around the forts with the top buttons of their jackets undone, trousers sagging onto their boot tops. The Army, however, never let them forget for long that they were military men and must appear as such. Accordingly, the soldier's life was punctuated by a steady and thoroughly detested round of inspections and other formal ceremonies characterized by the proverbial Army spit and polish. And indeed when the men lined up on the parade ground in full-dress uniforms, they were as stiffly elegant as any soldiers in the world.

The lithographs at right and on the following four pages, reproduced from the 1882 edition of the Army clothing regulations *(above)*, confirm the splendor of military dress during the Indian wars. An artillery private's dress blues *(page 44)* sported such embellishments as helmet plumes, with scarlet trim, cording and tassels on the jackets. The humble infantryman's helmet sprouted a fierce brass spike *(page 42)*. (So obviously Prussian was the inspiration for the spike that when the American military attaché in Paris wore one of them just after the Franco-Prussian war of 1870, he was threatened by a mob.)

The dress uniforms may have been ornate, but they were also descriptive: from them one could tell a great deal about the wearer. Details such as the color of helmet cords and cuff tabs, trouser stripes and the enlisted man's chevrons or the officer's insignia conveyed an instant message about a soldier's rank, his skills and even his duties in the Army. To the trained eye, the uniform was as easy to read as a book.

SERGEANT MAJOR OF CAVALRY (FULL DRESS)

Sergeant major was the most powerful rank below that of officer. The yellow trimming on his helmet, jacket and trousers proclaims this imposing fellow to be a cavalryman.

PRIVATE OF CAVALRY (FULL DRESS)

Though this soldier's uniform is topped by a spectacular dyed-horsehair helmet plume, he lacks a trouser stripe, making it instantly evident that he is neither officer nor sergeant.

SERGEANT OF SIGNAL CORPS (FULL DRESS)

The pair of embroidered signal flags at the center of this sergeant's chevrons, together with the orange trim on his coat, trousers and helmet, indicate his branch of service.

PRIVATE OF INFANTRY (FULL DRESS)

While artillerymen and cavalrymen buckled on swords as part of their dress uniform, this lowly foot soldier was required to carry a cumbersome 45/70 single-shot rifle.

ARTILLERY FATIGUE DRESS AND SUMMER HELMET

The white cork helmet, issued to soldiers in the Southwest after 1882, was cordially despised; they claimed that it made them conspicuous targets for Indian sharpshooters.

CAVALRYMAN (IN CAMPAIGN HAT AND STABLE FROCK)

Though cavalrymen had little affection for the baggy coat and trousers prescribed for stable duty, the soft, broad-brimmed campaign hat was a favorite throughout the West.

PRIVATE OF LIGHT ARTILLERY (FULL DRESS)

The scarlet trim on his uniform is the clue to this soldier's branch of service. The swords some men carried with their dress uniforms measured three and a half feet in length.

MUSICIAN OF HEAVY ARTILLERY (FULL DRESS)

Three things identify this man's job: the stripes across the front of his jacket, the double stripes down the sides of his trousers and — of course — the brass bugle that he carries.

CAPTAIN OF CAVALRY (FULL DRESS)

Cascading plumes of dyed buffalo hair help to give this gray-mustached junior officer the aspect of a Victorian cavalier. The long, double-breasted frock coat was for officers only.

MAJOR GENERAL (FULL DRESS)

The dress uniform for generals included — besides the golden epaulets and a dignified sash — a dashing Napoleonic hat (appropriately called a chapeau) with an ornament on one side.

A long pile of cordwood near the post trader's compound at Fort Robinson bespeaks the severity of Nebraska winters.

2 | A mixed bag of Western forts

The uniformity of most government issue did not apply to the hundreds of forts that guarded the frontier. Although life on the posts followed a fixed and monotonous routine, the forts themselves were unique in appearance and constantly changing. Built of whatever material was nearest at hand, some were the epitome of ramshackle misery and others approached opulence.

In the 1870s, Fort Robinson in Nebraska (below) was transformed from a tent camp to a community of solid structures when it became apparent that a permanent military command was needed to oversee the disgruntled Sioux of the Red Cloud Agency there. The officers' quarters were adobe, but most of the other buildings — barracks, shops, stables, the guardhouse and post trader's store — were constructed of logs chinked with a mixture of mud, sand and lime. A dozen years later, some of these huts would be replaced by splendid frame structures (pages 54-55).

But in one aspect, at least, Fort Robinson was typical of Western posts built after 1870. It had no outer wall; its only stockade was an interior one, built to protect the post trader's goods from light-fingered soldiers. Most frontier commanders agreed with the general in Dakota Territory who said: "It is better for troop morale to depend on vigilance and breechloaders for protection than to hide behind palisades."

47

An enlisted man with a pet dog surveys the imposing sprawl of Fort Thomas, erected in the desolate Arizona desert in 1876.

Constructed of adobe and brick, Fort Union, New Mexico, nevertheless kept precautionary fire-fighting gear in readiness *(center)*.

Fort Riley in Kansas, built to consolidate several lesser posts, boasted a mess hall that could seat about 2,000 men.

53

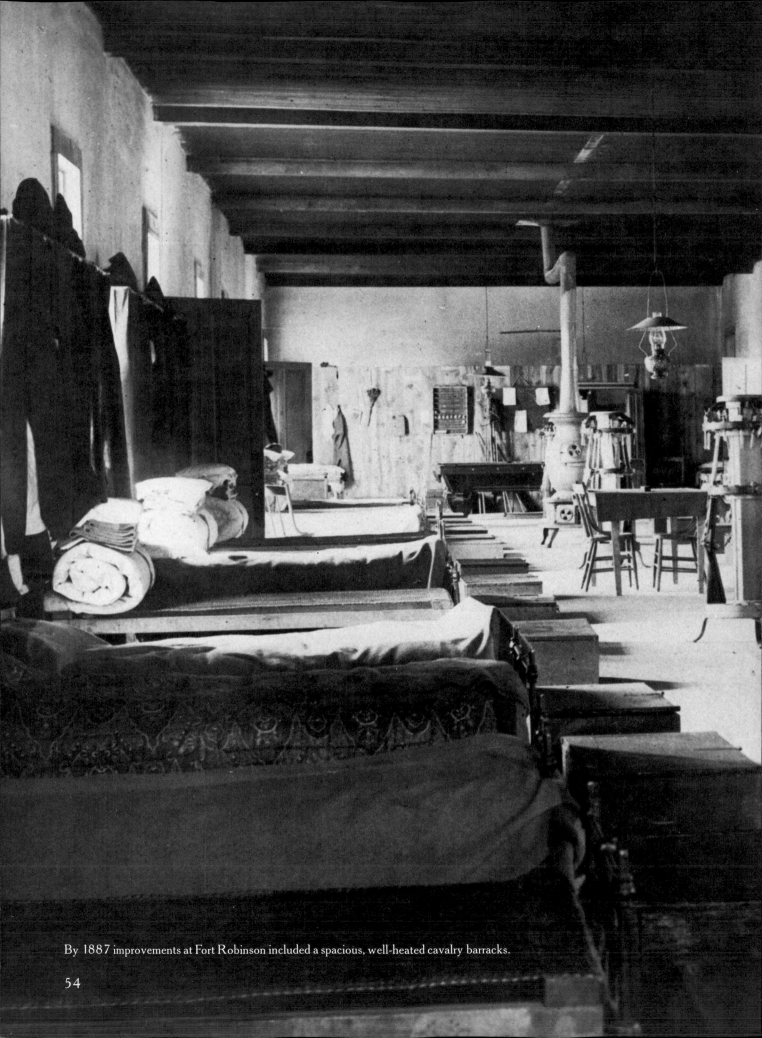

By 1887 improvements at Fort Robinson included a spacious, well-heated cavalry barracks.

The "glittering misery" of the soldier's home

A frontier soldier might spend up to half of any given year on campaign against the Indians, which meant that he spent the rest of his time on post. Every soldier was glad to reach a refuge after weeks of months in the field, but few regarded a fort as a pleasant place to come home to. True, the site of a fort had to meet certain physical requirements: there had to be enough water to sustain a regiment or a few companies, sufficient grass for animals, some timber for building and fuel, and a space of level terrain that could encompass barracks, officers' quarters, storehouses, stables, wagon sheds and a parade ground. But strategic necessity, rather than comfort, was the prime consideration in the placement of the garrisons. Their function was to guard transportation routes — primarily wagon trails and the new railroads being built across the West — and to keep watch over the always volatile Indians. By their very nature, most Army posts lay far from civilization, often deep in a land of "hostiles," as the Army called unfriendly Indians.

Danger was never far away. Although Indians were generally sensible enough not to attempt a frontal assault on an Army post, they sometimes made sudden raids on the horses or other livestock that grazed off post under a light guard during the day; on a number of occasions the men guarding the animals were killed before a rescue party could reach them. Indians frequently ambushed soldiers dispatched off post on short details to cut wood or bring in water. And a soldier who went out alone might be taking his life in his hands. In 1866

a soldier named Blair ventured out from Fort Reno, Wyoming, to skin a wolf killed by poisoned bait. As one of his comrades recalled, six Indians dashed out of a gully near the fort, "filled Blair with arrows, took his scalp, and then tomahawked him right before our eyes."

Yet some soldiers actually expressed a wish for an Indian attack. This was mostly the boastful talk of new recruits, but even veterans sometimes requested escort or courier duty that might take them through dangerous country. Such requests were prompted not so much by courage as by a desire for escape from the monotony, hardships and drudgery of the fort itself.

The amenities of a typical early frontier fort were minimal. Officers occupied private quarters, usually in a row of small houses where each officer had two to four rooms, but enlisted men were crammed into barracks where rows of bunks or cots stood head-in to walls. Major George Forsyth described some typical barracks as "too small, poorly constructed, illy ventilated, frequently overcrowded, generally cold in winter, hot in summer." Candles provided flickering gleams of light, and a round iron stove offered a tiny circle of warmth in an all-enveloping atmosphere of draft and chill. Senior enlisted men had the best places, near windows in summer, near stoves in winter. Ranking noncoms such as sergeants had the luxury of small rooms next to barrack rooms — and a luxury they were. Forsyth, a soldier to the core, believed lack of privacy was one of the central hardships of life on a frontier post.

Privies were outside and bathhouses were virtually nonexistent. Although War Department orders stipulated that each man should take a bath once a week, one officer pointed out the paradox: "The regulations say the men must be made to bathe frequently; the doctors say it should be done; the men want to do it; the company officers wish them to do so; the Quartermasters' Department says it is important. Yet we have

In the late 1880s Private C. C. Chrisman sketched in his diary these vignettes of a soldier's life at a fort in the Southwest. The drawings show: 1. Drill; 2. Kitchen police; 3. Post cleanup; 4. Construction detail; 5. Guard duty; 6. The guardhouse.

no bathrooms." In 1878, in fact, one officer remembered that during his 30 years in the Army he had never seen a bathhouse at any post. And even when facilities were available, few Southwestern posts had water to spare for weekly baths. It wasn't so bad after a while, one soldier said; since everybody smelled they all got used to one another.

In the Southwest, posts were particularly uncomfortable in summer. The men obtained a measure of relief from the heat by hanging large clay jars called ollas both inside and outside the barracks to keep their water cool. The water in the ollas evaporated rapidly in the heat, providing a rude form of air-conditioning. In front of their quarters to protect themselves from the sun, soldiers erected structures called ramadas, constructed of saplings and covered with leafy brush. As a young cavalry officer, John G. Bourke wrote, the ramadas offered "a modicum of shelter from the fierce shafts of a sun which shone not to warm and enlighten, but to enervate and kill."

Southwestern posts also were afflicted with centipedes, scorpions, tarantulas and snakes. One veteran described Fort Grant in Arizona as "the place where everything that grows pricks and everything that breathes bites." The outraged wife of a lieutenant stationed at Camp Supply in Indian Territory (later the state of Oklahoma) wrote: "This country itself is bad enough and the location of the post is most unfortunate, but to compel officers and men to live in these old huts of decaying, moldy wood, which are reeking with malaria and alive with bugs, and perhaps snakes, is wicked." At Camp Supply, in 1869, officers' quarters and barracks alike had damp earthen floors that daily sprouted crops of mushrooms and toadstools.

The early forts on the northern Plains were, if anything, worse. Many of them were infested with rats, mice and insects. Fine dust blew through cracks in the log or adobe walls and log roofs of the buildings in summer, and snow sifted through in winter. When Colonel Delos B. Sackett inspected the forts of the Missouri River country in 1866, he found many of the buildings uninhabitable. At one ramshackle post in Dakota Territory every single structure was worthless, he said, with the possible exception of the flagstaff, and that was only "tolerable." At Fort Randall the cottonwood-log buildings were so full of rats and other vermin that the men

preferred to sleep outdoors. While sitting in the commanding officer's quarters, Sackett recalled, "two bugs dropped from the ceiling on me."

As time went on, the forts were improved. Log or adobe structures were replaced by frame, stone, concrete or brick buildings. Mess halls were painted, bunks were equipped with springs and cotton mattresses, kerosene lamps replaced candles. Officers were given two-story frame houses with well-tended lawns in front. But one thing never changed—the routine of Army life.

On a typical day at one post in Dakota Territory, reveille blew at 5:30. First drill was held at 6:15, fall-out for fatigue duty was signaled at 7:30, guard mount took place at 8:30, afternoon fatigue commenced at 1:00, drill at 4:30 and taps sounded at 8:15 that evening. And woe betide the man who missed any of the calls established by his commanding officer and the War Department back in Washington.

Some Army wives professed to see romance and excitement in the activities of a post. One lieutenant's wife wrote: "We lived, ate, slept by the bugle calls." She had a special affection for "the beautiful stable-call for the cavalry, when the horses are groomed and watered, the thrilling fire-call and the startling assembly, or call-to-arms, when every soldier jumps for his rifle and every officer buckles on his sword, and a woman's heart stands still." Indeed there was panoply and pageant, but the same lady once remarked that Army life was really "glittering misery."

From daily experience, most soldiers knew well that the misery far outweighed the glitter. The fatigue details that took up a large part of the day called for a variety of tedious work. Off-post details built roads and bridges, and repaired telegraph lines. Woodcutting parties often went miles in search of fuel, looking over their shoulders for signs of hostiles. Other groups escorted recruits, paymasters, mail carriers or emigrant trains to and from the post. Water parties filled barrels around the post. This was a particularly detested assignment during the fierce winters of the northern Plains, as was the task of sawing ice for summer use. And there were endless police details on post to dispose of garbage, clean up stables and other buildings, cultivate the post garden or weed the parade ground.

Guard mount, the most important event of an average day, was a particularly exacting and inexorable rit-

Three post gardeners display their vegetables at Fort Assinniboine, Montana. Gardeners were released from fatigue duties since, as one Army wife declared, "over a plebeian cabbage we have had a real feast."

ual. Even when Fort Phil Kearny, Wyoming, was under siege in 1866, men turned out for guard mount with freshly blackened shoes, polished buttons and sponged uniforms. At the sound of a bugle call, the men assigned to guard duty assembled in front of their barracks for inspection by the company first sergeant. At a second call 10 minutes later they were then marched to the parade ground and inspected by the sergeant major, who announced assignments to various points around the post. Then the men were turned over to the officer of the day, who inspected them again and put them through manual-of-arms drill. The proper passwords were exchanged between officers, and the men were finally marched to the guardhouse, the base of operations for their two-hour tours of sentry duty.

The best-turned-out man at guard mount was selected as the commanding officer's orderly for the day —a much-coveted assignment, for the orderly was excused from guard duty and fatigue details and could loaf in the post headquarters when not carrying messages. Trumpeter Ami F. Mulford of the 7th Cavalry once suggested that an orderly never had to do "much

of anything but buzz the hired girl in the kitchen, and eat up all the cold victuals he could find. This was called 'dog robbing,' —a very suitable name!" And beyond these pleasant advantages for the soldier lucky enough to be chosen, the job reflected honor upon himself, his company and his captain.

On one occasion when General Phil Sheridan visited Fort Rice, Dakota Territory, competition to serve as his orderly was keen among the sergeants at the post. Sergeant Ralph Donath represented a company of the 17th Infantry. The contest finally narrowed down to him and a sergeant from the 7th Cavalry. The officer of the day could not decide which of them was better turned out, and finally ordered them to remove belts, blouses and shoes. "Thus ended the competition," Sergeant Donath recalled, "as the cavalry Sergt. had on civilian stockings and I had on the regulation ones." Donath was an old Army hand. Normally, he himself wore civilian socks, but in a competition like that one, he didn't miss a trick.

Companies were supposed to assemble every day to drill, if the weather permitted. This official policy, however, was widely ignored, often because Western posts were undermanned. As late as 1878 one lieutenant declared that "one half the posts of the Army have no drills. The companies are so small that all the men are occupied in taking care of the post." Though a few officers —notably that proud martinet George Armstrong Custer —turned their troops into good riders and excellent shots, many others simply did not care about the prosaic task of training their men. Such indifference stemmed partly from an ill-founded opinion that Indians were unskilled in the martial arts and that chasing after a bunch of savages was an almost insulting comedown after the glorious setpiece battles of the Civil War.

Target practice was given especially short shrift until the late 1870s; even when officers wanted to ready their men for combat, the posts sometimes did not have spare ammunition for small-arms and artillery practice. Owing to a lack of ammunition, the 18th Infantry held no target practice at all in 1866, although it was located squarely in the country of hostile Cheyennes and Sioux. When ammunition was available it was sometimes considered too expensive to use in target practice. When the 7th Cavalry was issued two new Gatling guns in Kansas in 1867, young Lieutenant E. S. God-

Fort Ruby: the worst post in the West

In their early stages, most military outposts were desolate places, but some were worse than others. During the seven years it existed, one post in particular was considered by its garrison the epitome of the frontier station at its worst. Fort Ruby, located midway between Salt Lake City, Utah, and Carson City, Nevada, was built in 1862 to protect the Overland Mail route from Paiute raiders. The nearest settlement was 120 miles away. The setting was grim; Colonel P. Edward Connor, the post's first commanding officer, called Ruby Valley "a bleak, inhospitable place—no forage nor lumber to build with." No lumber, that is, for anything more grand than log cabins *(below)*, while horses had to be grazed over a wide area for lack of forage.

A measure of the state of morale at Ruby at the outset was the garrison's desperate offer to forgo a total of $30,000 back pay if only Washington would order the regiment East to fight in the Civil War. Washington refused. Two years later, a single ray of sunshine graced Ruby when a distillery was built nearby, marketing a fiery product called "Old Commissary." However much that beverage lifted morale in the ranks, it was simply not enough. When Captain George Walker was given command of Ruby in 1867, his first act was to take six months' furlough.

In 1869, with the construction of the railroad to carry the mail, the Army closed Fort Ruby. This happy action, however, did not come soon enough to avoid a final scandal—the court-martial of Ruby's last commandant, Captain Timothy Connelly, for having embezzled the company funds.

In 1868, Fort Ruby's finest building was the officers' quarters of hewn logs and mud daubing. A year later Ruby was abandoned.

frey had to face the problem of training crews to man them. "I wanted to have target practice," he later recalled, "but was told I would have to pay for the ammunition. The commanding officer refused to authorize target practice for fear he would have to pay for the ammunition." The crews never got to fire those Gatlings.

Cavalry drills showed an unfortunate misplacement of emphasis. Some horses were better trained than their riders and learned commands so well that, when a trooper fell off, an old drill horse would often continue riderless through the routine without a mistake. But the men were given little instruction in the art of mounting and guiding the animal. Cavalry recruits were simply expected to get on and ride — with predictable results. One commander, understating the case, noted that in horsemanship, recruits were "but clumsy children compared with the Indians."

There was fairly constant processing of new horses as well as new soldiers, and these were times of great merriment for all but the hapless rider. Ami Mulford recalled climbing aboard a saddled Army horse for the first time and finding that the stirrups had been crossed so that his knees were pushed up against his chin. The horse, a wise old veteran, "puts on a horse grin and gets down to business," wrote Mulford. Off they went, the rider bouncing in the saddle, tumbling off, remounting and repeating the cycle for a good hour. When at last he was allowed to dismount, the horse played its part to the end: "As I turned away from the head of the horse, back went its ears, and with a quick swing it lunged forward and took a not very gentle nip where saddle blisters were already in evidence, and held on. With a jerk that almost tears away the seat of my trousers, I break away; my initiation drill is over, and I meander down the Company street, tired, discouraged, mad, homesick."

Near the men's quarters at Fort Grant, Arizona, there was a sandy spot on a riverbed where horses were broken to the saddle. Captain John Bourke, one of some 40,000 Irishmen who served during the Indian wars, re-created the spectacle with all the glee and narrative skill of a born storyteller: "Such squealing and struggling and biting and kicking, and rolling in the dust and getting up again never could be seen outside of a herd of California 'broncos.' The animal was first thrown, blindfolded, and then the bridle and saddle were put on,

the latter girthed so tightly that the horse's eyes would start from their sockets.

"If there were many horses arriving in a 'bunch,' there would be lots of fun and no little danger and excitement. The men would mount and amid the encouraging comments of the on-lookers begin the task of subjugation. The bronco nearly always looked around and up at his rider with an expression of countenance that was really benignant, and then he would roach his back, get his four feet bunched together and await developments. If the rider foolishly listened to his critics, he would almost always mistake this temporary paroxysm of docility for fear or lack of spirit.

"And then would come the counsel, inspired by the Evil One himself: 'Arrah, thin, shtick yer sphurs int' him, Moriarty.'

"No sooner would the rowels strike his flanks than the air would seem to be filled with a mass of mane and tail rapidly revolving, and of hoofs flying out in defiance of all the laws of gravity, while a descendant of the kings of Ireland, describing a parabolic orbit through space, would shoot like a meteor into the sand and plough it up with his chin."

Once broken, a horse was usually assigned to a specific rider, and cavalrymen developed great affection for their mounts. George Armstrong Custer once issued a directive switching men and horses so that each company would ride horses of a single color, presenting the sort of snappy parade appearance that appealed to the golden-haired colonel of the 7th Cavalry. His men deeply resented the insensitive order.

The depth of regard that soldiers felt for their horses is measured by the reaction of a cavalryman whose mount was hit in battle. "I found that Sam was shot through the bowels. I unsaddled him and turned him loose to die, but he followed me like a dog and would put his head against me and push, groaning like a person. I was forced to shoot him to end his misery. I had to try two or three times before I could do it. He kept looking at me with his great brown eyes. When I did fire he never knew what hurt him. He was a splendid horse, and could do his mile in 1.57."

The shared rigors that made a man feel so close to a horse forged far stronger bonds of friendship between man and man. New recruits paired informally with a "bunky" — most often another new man — and they

61

Attended by a stern enlisted man, an officer's family takes the air at Fort Shaw, called "the Queen of Montana Forts" for such amenities as shade trees and clipped lawns.

63

might literally have to share one bunk; not until the mid-1870s were men generally assured of single beds. In the field bunkies shared food and blankets, and usually fought side by side. Inevitably they became confidants, sharing their life stories and their hopes and fears.

If a soldier had any family feeling it was usually for his company, typically comprising about 40 or 50 men and one or two officers. Soldiers almost always served out their entire hitch in the same company, even if they enlisted more than once. The members of a company lived together, fought together, drilled together and possessed a high degree of self-sufficiency. A company could sell part of its rations to buy food not available at the post commissary, and these funds were sometimes used for improvements in the men's quarters or for recreation. Every company appointed its own tailor, barber and often a company cobbler; some cavalry companies had their own blacksmiths, who got extra pay for their work. Even in quiet moments, a company operated as a unit, competing against the other companies at horseshoes, boxing, baseball and horse racing.

The sense of loyalty generated by the self-contained nature of a company was reinforced by the permanence of its location and its officers. The transfer of officers was extremely rare, and many companies came to be known by their captains' names, rather than by their official designation letters. And because there was no fixed system of rotating troops on the frontier (it was considered too expensive) men were often stuck in the same remote areas for years on end.

If officers gave the orders and soldiers carried them out, first sergeants made it all go. An enlisted man could not even speak to an officer without obtaining his first sergeant's permission. Describing the prerogatives of his position, First Sergeant H. H. McConnell of the 6th Cavalry said, "The First Sergeant is virtually in command of the company, and if he but conduct himself as he should, he can command the respect of both officers and men, and lives as comfortably as he wishes to. He messes by himself, has his horse cared for by the men, has his own quarters, and it only depends on himself and his capabilities as to his comfort and success."

Noncommissioned officers were often popular with their men, but they had to be tough. During the Indian wars, most of them were Civil War veterans, older and wiser than most enlisted men and often picked for their abilities to maintain order. "Old Sergeant McMakin was a Civil War vet," recalled one former 17th Infantry soldier, "and he was mean as hell." Some noncommissioned officers disciplined men with their fists; some were simply brawlers, off duty and on. This sort of noncom was often in trouble. If he was broken to the ranks, he had occasion to regret his tyrannies when he found himself as a private among men he had bullied on another day. But he usually regained his stripes quickly, for his services were necessary.

The violent discipline meted out in the frontier Army often begat violent responses. Sometimes the bodies of sergeants were found, apparently killed by their own men. In 1870 an officer was caned to death while trying to arrest three drunken soldiers in Austin, Texas. Another officer once saw a man lagging in formation and whipped him back into place with the flat of his saber. Later the soldier fell back again; when the officer reappeared, the man aimed his rifle at his superior's heart and pulled the trigger — but the rifle misfired. And still another officer gave two quarreling men bullwhips and ordered them to lash each other. Such punishment was illegal, but soldiers had little or no recourse.

Army discipline rankled not only because it was harsh but because the officers who meted it out often seemed themselves to be immune to it. One first sergeant commented in 1867: "I have seen officers more than once too drunk to perform their duty go unpunished, when the poor private would be fined and confined for the same offense without fail."

Soldiers saw themselves as victims of a vicious, unfeeling system, not only because of the discipline but because of their treatment generally. "None but a menial Cur," wrote one man at Camp Brown, Wyoming, "would stand the usage of a soldier of the Army of today in America." Some of the bitterest soldier complaints concerned that most fundamental of human needs — food. Army regulations called for each company to designate privates to serve in rotation as cooks. In principle, the idea was sound: the Army wanted its men to learn to cook on post so that they could prepare their own meals in the field. But in practice the system proved dreadful. Few soldiers knew even the rudiments of cooking; not until the Indian wars were over did the Army train men to cook and assign them to serve in

Dr.   Lieut. Moore.   Cr.

1864

April	14	To 6 prs ½ hose 37½	2 25		By Balance 352	177 39
"	"	2 Shirts	8 00			
	15	" Tobacco	50			
	16	" 1 Bridle order Mey	3 00			
"	"	1 pr Spurs	2 00			
	18	" 1 Bot Whiskey	1 50			
"	"	3 Cans Oysters	4 50			
			2 75			
	23	" 1 Comb	50			
	25	" 1 Gall Whiskey	6 00		To amt Brot up	127 88
"	"	2 Cans Oysters	3 00	June 4	" Cash	2 50
	26	1 " Do.	1 50	" "	Buttons	50
	29	" 1 Piece Soap	50	" "	1 pr Shoes	3 50
"	"	1 pr Gauntlets	3 50	7 "	1 Can Oysters	1 50
	30	" Paid order	5			125 88
"	"	1 Bot Whiskey	1 50	13 "	1 Bot Wine	3 00
May	2	" 1 Pitcher	75	16 "	1 Cant Whiskey	
"	"	6 Tumblers	3 00		pr. order	2 00
"	"	6 Cans Oysters	8 00	18 "	1 Can Oysters	1 50
"	"	1 pr. Pants	12	" "	Tobacco	25
	3	" Cash	10 00	20 "	2 Bot Champaigne	6 00
	7	" pd Lt. Lewis	2 36	" "	Tobacco	38
	9	" 10 yds Calico	3 75	23 "	1 plug Tobacco	50
"	"	4 " Bl. Cot	2 00	" "	Oysters	1 50
"	"	Thread	13	24 "	1 Pipe	7 50
	18	" 1 Cap	5 00	28 "	Cash	5 00
	23	" 1 Chest Lock	50	" "	1 pt. Whiskey	1 50
"	"	1 Can Oysters	1 50	30 "	Tobacco	38
	25	" Blkg.	13	July 5 "	Do.	1 25
	26	" 1 Can Oysters	1 50	" "	1 Bot Wine	3 00
	30	" Candy	38	" "	1 " "	3 00
"	"	1 pr. Boots	10 00	" "	Tobacco	13
"	"	1 Bot. Pomade	37	6 "	1 Bot Ale	1 50
	31	" 1 " Brandy	2 00	" "	1 do Fine Tobacco	1 50
			127 88	7 "	1 Bot Ale	1 50
				8 "	Lace	12
						177 89
						177 39

that capacity. A standing joke among enlisted men was that cooks killed more soldiers than the Indians did.

Moreover, even if a man developed culinary talents, the food that the company cooks had to work with was maddeningly monotonous. The staples consisted of beans, hardtack, bacon, flour, coffee, coarse bread, occasional low-grade range beef and even more occasional game, plus such condiments as salt, brown sugar, vinegar and molasses. One sergeant gave this description of a typical day's meals: "For breakfast we had beef hash, dry sliced bread (no butter) and coffee (no milk); for dinner, sliced beef, dry bread and coffee, for supper, coffee straight — just dry bread and coffee." He summed it all up with simple accuracy: "The food was very poor." Nevertheless, it was better than what a soldier could expect on campaign. When one recruit reported to Company M of the 7th Cavalry, a friendly veteran told him: "It is a good plan to feed up to the limit when you get a chance, for you will need a hump like a camel, to draw on, when you get in the field."

Improper storage of food compounded the dietary problems. Bacon sometimes arrived on a post rotten

and green or yellow. A soldier noted that one shipment was so spoiled that the "fat had commenced to sluff off from the lean, and it was ⅗ inches thick—also full of mice, as was the flour." Another soldier said of bacon served at Fort Phil Kearny that it "would have killed the men if it had not been thoroughly boiled."

Hardtack was presumed to be edible, remarked one man, if it was "light brown with holes in it like those in soda crackers, and rather brittle." Unfortunately it was not always so. In fact, continued one soldier, the hardtack given him at Fort Laramie "was dark and stale. It was hard, so that when I tried to bite it I could not make the least impression on the unruly stuff. Holding it in the palm of my left hand I struck it with my right fist, but only succeeded in skinning my knuckles. Then I tried to break it in two by holding it in both hands, as I had formerly broken apples, but it resisted like a rod. Then I brought it down hard on my knee several times, but only bruised my knee."

"Did you ever attempt to eat a hardtack!" exclaimed Trumpeter Mulford. "If not, try to bite a piece out of an old fire-brick. I do not wonder," he continued, "the

A cavalry troop drills at Fort Custer, Montana. Even men who enjoyed riding hated drilling an hour and a half a day, six days a week.

Government examines a man's teeth so carefully before he is enlisted; it should provide steel teeth and a file with which to sharpen them."

Even the water could be foul. Custer's wife remembered waiting for Missouri River mud to settle in her glass before drinking it. She learned to settle the mud with alum and then to accept the taste. Of a similar stream aptly named the Little Muddy, Mulford observed that the only way to get a drink "is to take a mouthful of the mixture, and squeeze the mud out in your mouth, and swallow the water."

Soldiers could not do much about the water, but they did their best to remedy other deficiencies in their diet. Every post tried to cultivate a kitchen garden, and wherever possible, companies also raised their own vegetables, competing with other companies to grow the best and most produce. Any surplus was sold to augment the company fund, and part of that fund went right back into the purchase of more plant seeds. But at many posts, agriculture was impossible because of poor soil or a shortage of water. And more than one garden detail watched helplessly as clouds of locusts or grasshoppers descended on crops that had been carefully cultivated through the summer months.

The bad diet—coupled with poor sanitation, a lack of bathing facilities, and an abundance of bedbugs and lice—made for a high rate of illness. Scurvy, caused by the Army's unpardonable failure to provide fresh fruit and vegetables in the diet, was rampant until the mid-1870s: in 1867 the commander of Fort Stevenson in Dakota Territory reported 51 of his 200 men down with scurvy and one death. That same year, when cholera broke out at Fort Wallace, Kansas, the medical officer reported that men debilitated by diet appeared particularly vulnerable to infection. Epidemics of influenza, diphtheria, smallpox, yellow fever and typhoid fever raged across whole posts. There were few drugs to treat these diseases. Doses of whiskey with quinine were specifics for nearly everything, and if that didn't work, a powerful purgative was administered.

Given all the miseries of life on post—low pay, poor living conditions, brutal and inequitable discipline, loneliness, monotony and the proximity of danger—it is hardly surprising that soldiers deserted in droves. "Toward spring," one soldier wrote, "the men began to desert." He made it sound like a vernal rite. As the weather grew warm, officers started holding roll calls at odd times of the day and night, ready to sound the alarm if a man were missing. There were ways around that tactic, however. One first sergeant had 30 men rationed and armed for detached duty; he marched them out of a Colorado post, set a furious pace for about 30 miles, then stopped, informed them they were all deserters and that it was every man for himself. Bidding them goodbye, he struck off for the mining regions.

A soldier named Farrelly is said to have resorted to an even more devious ploy to get out of the Army—one that has come down in military mythology in a number of variations. Disenchanted with Army life, Farrelly began feigning insanity, singing at the top of his lungs while on guard, addressing officers by their given names and displaying other signs of derangement. When he began spending hours on the parade ground with a fishing line in his hands, muttering to himself, medical officers finally decided that he had to be discharged. The day he received the discharge papers, he met his commanding officer on the parade ground. "Ah! Farrelly," said the officer, "why aren't you fishing this morning?" Holding up the papers, Farrelly replied, "I've got what I was fishing for this long time."

The bulk of those who deserted left within their first year of service. Many of them were recruits who had signed up in hard times, when jobs were scarce and Army pay plus room and board looked highly attractive. But that Army pay was both deceptive and disappointing. Originally $16 a month, it was reduced to $13 in 1871, and soldiers did not even get the purchasing power of that miserly amount. The Army paid its men in paper currency; on the frontier, paper money usually had to be converted to gold or silver coin before it could be spent, and, in any case, the paper bills were discounted from 15 to 40 per cent. Naturally enough, then, desertions invariably increased when economic conditions improved. Men who went over the hill usually took along their horse, rifle and other equipment, which would bring from $150 to $300 on the frontier. Occasionally a furious officer would chase after deserters, but usually a man on the run was safe if he could get far enough away.

Yet most men stayed on, at least for the full term of their first five-year enlistment. Many sergeants in the 1880s had 25 years of service to their credit. The

The heavy hand of frontier discipline

Commenting on the standards of discipline in the frontier Army, one sergeant declared that "as long as you behaved yourself and performed your duty as a soldier, you got along all right." That was doubtless true, as far as it went. The fact is that few enlisted men served out their hitch without being accused of some sort of infraction. And since legal punishment for any breach of conduct, no matter how small, required a court-martial, the number of military trials was staggering: in one year during the Indian wars 2,056 trials were held in the Department of the Platte, which was then manned by only 3,008 soldiers.

Punishment was generally harsh and arbitrary. Men who committed minor infractions, such as sleeping through roll call, might be fined a month's pay or spend up to a month in the guardhouse or both. Custer incarcerated such offenders in a special prison of his own design—a 15-foot-deep hole in the ground covered with boards. A soldier found guilty of drunkenness or insubordination might have to march all day carrying a 30- or 40-pound log; he might even be strung up by his wrists or thumbs. A deserter could be compelled to wear a 25-pound ball and chain around his ankle for months.

Yet a man subjected to such disciplinary measures might count himself lucky, for Army regulations then recommended the death penalty for at least 12 crimes, including striking an officer and sleeping on guard duty.

Heavy penalties and the lack of legal recourse were largely responsible for a desertion rate that approximated one third of all the soldiers recruited during the Indian wars. When the government made a survey of some captured deserters, most of them said they had fled "tyrannical superiors."

At Fort Grant, Arizona, men found guilty of minor offenses chop wood under armed guard. They spent their nights in the guardhouse.

On a day of subzero cold, a guard detail at Fort Keogh, Montana, makes its rounds in government-issue buffalo coats, fur gauntlets and muskrat hats. In the worst weather, the men might add wool face masks.

number of men with long service records tended to rise toward the end of the Indian wars, owing in part to a gradual amelioration of living conditions, in part to a waning of the Indian danger. Some soldiers stayed because they knew no other way of life and had no home other than the fort. A few supplemented their Army pay with additional sums extended to skilled extra-duty artisans; an Army carpenter, for example, got 35 cents a day over and above his regular Army wages. And there were those who found that, on balance, life on the Western posts could be tolerable and occasionally even enjoyable, provided one had a thick skin, an iron constitution and a taste for simple diversions.

During the evening at least, and at times during the day, relaxation was available. In the barrack rooms, soldiers played cards, told stories and sang their favorite tunes, often accompanied by someone in the company who could play a banjo, guitar, harmonica or accordion. More professional fare occasionally turned up at some of the larger posts: touring minstrel groups passed through from time to time; and if the fort was a regimental headquarters, the regimental band ordinarily played for an hour each evening.

For the most part, however, soldiers created their own amusements. Many companies held dances for the enlisted men every two months or so, and some went so far as to put on minstrel shows and theatricals, but the staple mode of fun on the Western posts was practical jokery. One 1st Cavalry soldier removed his Army-issue belt buckle, which bore the large, raised letters "US," and covered the letters with red ink. He then stamped the "US" on his hip, and informed rookies that they were to be branded with a hot iron, proving it by dropping his trousers and showing them his own brand. (The recruits had good reason to be fooled by this joke; until 1874, Army regulations permitted branding and tattooing of deserters.)

Clarence Gould, another 1st Cavalryman, recounted an elaborate prank devised by soldiers at Fort Assinniboine, Montana Territory. "One night in the dead of winter and just before taps," he recalled, "one of the men came to the orderly room and told 1st Sgt. Hawks there was an Indian squaw out back. Hawks immediately investigated, found the facts to be as stated, and suggested to the squaw that it was warmer in his quarters, but something went wrong with his plans, for the Indian announced in gutteral English: 'Me no squaw, me buck!' and drew a butcher knife from his blanket and commenced cutting circles in the air too close to Hawks's head for comfort. It is needless to state that top pusher made the orderly room in ten seconds flat." The sergeant never did know "that his Indian friend was none other than Shorty Grant, a Trumpeter of his own troop, and the knife was a long-bladed breadknife from the troop kitchen."

When soldiers felt a need for diversion of a calmer sort, reading matter of some kind was usually available. A number of posts had libraries, sometimes surprisingly extensive. The Fort Sully library had 800 volumes and offered such periodicals as *The London Punch, Appleton's Weekly* and *North American Review.*

Even the most forlorn posts offered one oasis—the sutler's or trader's store. (Sutlers were merchants licensed to travel with specific regiments; in 1867 they were replaced by franchised traders who set up permanent stores at Army posts.) There, men bought whiskey, beer, tobacco, canned fruit—especially to satisfy their craving for a change of diet—and canned meat and other food when they were just hungry. The stores also offered such pragmatic items as shoelaces, needles and thread, combs and soap.

In separate and segregated rooms for officers and men, the sutlers and traders provided their own forms of recreation. One officer fondly recalled the sutler's establishment at his Arizona post as having "a cool pleasant room, with a minimum of flies, the latest papers, perfect quiet, genial companionship, cool water in ollas swinging from the rafters, and covered by boards upon which in a thin layer of soil, grew a picturesque mantle of green barley, and, on a table conveniently near, cans of lemon-sugar, tumblers and spoons and one or two packs of cards." Many of these establishments supplied billiard tables as well as cards and there usually was gambling, although Army regulations forbade it.

The sutler or post trader commonly extended credit to the traditionally improvident soldiers: The expenditures of enlisted men were later deducted from their pay; officers, who were considered better risks, were allowed to run up personal tabs as a privilege of rank. The credit system was essential, if only because payday was often irregular. Theoretically, it came every two months, assuming that hostiles had not cut off the post

for protracted periods and that nothing had happened to the paymaster en route. One solder likened the arrival of the paymaster to the appearance of an angel; it seemed just as miraculous. An officer in Texas remarked that six or eight months frequently passed between paydays. He added that when pay arrived, the money was quickly spent and then "the camp would relapse into its normal and impecunious condition." With their currency gone, the men would exchange tobacco, articles of clothing and cartridges as a monetary medium. (These last two items were bartered in violation of Army regulations.)

But some men actually managed to save money out of their meager wages. A soldier with $1,500 in his pocket rode into Billings, Montana, one day and bought several city lots — an act the local paper thought showed a touching and sensible faith in the town's future. But on payday, most soldiers set out to drink their pockets dry at the sutler's. By the next day the hospital was full of "payday casualties." Some officers were particularly notorious drinkers, which did little to encourage temperance among their men. In the 1880s no less than four per cent of American soldiers were hospitalized as alcoholics — and this was a period when a man had to be in advanced delirium tremens or a condition equally grave in order to qualify for treatment.

Beginning in 1881 the sale of liquor on post was prohibited. Far from reducing alcoholism, this action

Cavalrymen on the target range look on intently as a private demonstrates the proper use of a carbine. Not until the 1800s did the Army institute regular target practice — and even then only 20 rounds per month.

produced an immediate efflorescence of off-post saloons, known as hog ranches. In addition to maintaining the steady flow of whiskey and beer, the hog ranches did a thriving trade in prostitution. The ladies of joy, as they were called, were not the most attractive available; cowboys, higher paid than the military, sneered at them as "soldiers' women." When a hog ranch appeared, venereal disease rates soared. Overall, some 8 per cent of all soldiers in the 1880s were infected.

Some commanders actually permitted prostitutes to live on post. And at some forts, unmarried women who were hired as company laundresses occasionally did more than launder. General Tasker Bliss once quoted a common Army belief that post doctors had "nothing to do but to confine laundresses and treat the clap." Some officers were understandably disenchanted with the laundress system. "Get rid of them!" urged Colonel R. I. Dodge in 1876. "It is an absurd continuation of a custom which grew out of other wants of the men of a company than washing clothes."

Most laundresses, however, were married to enlisted men and noncoms. They earned their meager wages —at Fort Boise, a laundress got five dollars a month for an officer's laundry and two dollars for an enlisted man's—and they were treated with the utmost respect. As one trooper of the 7th Cavalry said, they "were ladies in every sense of the word." Aside from doing the laundry of her husband's company, serving as midwife when an officer's lady was in labor and occasionally nursing the sick, there was not much to occupy such a woman. Women regularly turned out every day to watch the ritual of guard mount because, as one of them said, all the women were "a little silly over brass buttons." But simply by establishing a female presence, they provided a vital leavening for the oppressively humdrum atmosphere of isolated frontier posts.

The leavening, unfortunately, was usually in short supply. Few men could afford to keep families on Army pay. Furthermore, the Army actively discouraged marriage. Married men who wanted to enlist had to have permission from the adjutant general's office; a man who was already in the Army and wanted to get married had to have the permission of his company commander. Permission was often denied, since the number of married enlisted men in a regiment was strictly governed by the need for laundresses. During the greater part of the

On a plain outside Fort Douglas, cannon crews endure an artillery drill. The dust, din and heat of such practices yielded little in the way of useful skills: Indians rarely presented a massed target for an artillery attack, and the average artilleryman was anything but a master. Even one sergeant confessed: "I was not adequately trained to handle the gun."

Indian wars, Army regulations—with a logic known only to the bureaucratic mind—stipulated a quota of one laundress to every 19 and a half men.

Lucky indeed was the enlisted man who had a wife at the Western forts, for he was permitted to sleep out of the barracks and take his meals at home. The fare might not be much better, but at least it was more competently prepared than the stuff served up by company cooks. Understandably, any eligible female who arrived on post instantly found herself courted by hordes of lonely soldiers. It was a constant complaint of officers' wives that they could not keep servant girls brought out from the East. In short order, the girl was married, and there went the maid. The officers' wives at Fort Abraham Lincoln attempted to deal with that problem by ordering the Eastern employment agencies to send out the most homely girls they could find. The agencies complied; the girls in the next contingent had faces that the ladies agreed only a mother could love. Not so; soldiers could love them as well, and the new crop was married within two months.

Because female servants were so difficult to find and keep, officers often hired soldiers as servants for their families. Called strikers, such soldier-servants could earn $5 or $10 a month for their work and were relieved of some of their routine duties. In 1870 this practice was made illegal, but it continued anyway. The competition for a good striker could be fierce. An officer's wife once acquired a striker who, miraculously, turned out to be an excellent cook. One day a general on the post transferred the man back to active duty —and the following day transferred him to cook's duty in his own personal kitchen.

The quarters assigned to officers' families were generally superior to those on "Suds Row," or "Sudsville," as the area assigned to married enlisted men and laundresses was called. But there was one major drawback: an officer's family could be evicted on short notice if a higher-ranking officer demanded the house—an old Army custom known as ranking out. The process could be ruthless. Mrs. Orsemus Boyd, wife of a lieutenant at Fort Clark, was forced by a bachelor captain to move from comfortable quarters into a house with one room and a detached kitchen. Her eviction took place only four weeks after she gave birth to a child; the baby and her two other children were sick with whooping cough and bronchitis at the time. Another woman, given only three hours' notice to turn over her home to a higher-ranking officer, ended up living in a two-room converted chicken house.

Aside from this element of insecurity, life on post could be quite pleasant for the wife of an officer. Since a striker or female servant took over many of the household chores, she had leisure time for sewing bees, tea parties, theatricals and—if the region was free of hostiles —such outdoor activities as riding, shooting and fishing. In winter, when the men had returned from campaigning, some posts enjoyed a steady round of card parties and dinners that were, according to the wife of an officer stationed at Fort Shaw, Montana Territory, "quite elegant formal affairs, beautifully served with dainty china and handsome silver." Dances were held frequently, and with ladies in such short supply on posts, no woman ever lacked a partner.

There was a good deal of flirting at these affairs, but seldom much more than that, for the Army code of honor was rigid. Custer told his wife that she could ride, walk or dance with anyone she pleased, but that she must never permit any one officer to become her "special cavalier." Major Marcus A. Reno, one of Custer's officers, committed a couple of indiscretions along these lines, and was court-martialed for them twice. The second time, he was dismissed from the service for "conduct unbecoming an officer and gentleman." This conduct included his having peeped through a parlor window at the daughter of a colonel while she was chatting with her parents.

Distinctions of rank exerted a ubiquitous influence on the lives of women on post, for the military caste system extended to the dependents. The wives of officers and enlisted men held separate parties, and often did not even talk to each other. Nevertheless, the colonel's lady and Judy O'Grady were sisters under the skin. Every Army wife was well aware of the threat to her husband that lay outside the post. When the trumpets sounded officers' call and company commanders gathered for orders, wives of officers and enlisted men alike waited in silent dread.

As a column moved out, the regimental band played the traditional "The Girl I Left Behind Me." After the men had gone—said Elizabeth Custer—the post became "as still as if death had set its seal upon the door."

After a respite from duty, Oklahoma soldiers dressed in civilian hunting clothes proudly display their admirable bag of wild turkeys.

Members of the Jefferson Barracks, Missouri, baseball club fall in for a team picture. Theirs was one of the first teams fielded by the Army.

A skating party of Army wives and children brightens the bleak winter landscape of Montana's Fort Keogh in the late 1880s.

Brightening drab lives with the feminine touch

The best allies that officers — and a few enlisted men — had in their struggle to endure the harsh conditions at frontier forts were their wives. Those spunky ladies not only provided the meager amenities of each day's routine, but also engineered the occasional good times that relieved the monotony.

On first arrival they often ran head on against some flint-hard facts of life in the Western Army. At a New Mex-ico post, one daintily bred New York belle put her new Oriental carpets on the dirt floor of her log cabin and hung elegant white curtains at the windows. Within a few days a rainstorm swept the district, and a tide of mud surged through her doors, leaving the cabin in filthy disarray.

Even in the face of such hardships, the Army women persevered. In winter they defied the Plains' arctic winds to promote skating parties like the one shown here. In summer they coaxed their husbands into the hot, dusty countryside for picnics. They organized sewing circles, card parties, musicales and amateur theater groups. They even took on the brass: at one fort, they appropriated the living room of the commanding officer, proceeded to decorate it with bayonets, swords and flags, and threw a full-scale military ball in it.

A soldier and his family take to the water in a man-made pond at Fort Grant, Arizona.

Sporting the latest in 1876 chic amid Arizona's towering cacti, Army wives settle their men down for a picnic in the scrubby underbrush.

A lieutenant plays a hose on neighborhood children in the front yard of an officer's home at Fort Sill, Oklahoma.

A sergeant and his lady cozy down for some reading aloud at Fort Stanton, New Mexico.

3 | On the campaign trail

During an 1874 reconnaissance expedition, a cavalry camp is strung out in a valley of Dakota Territory's Black Hills.

For Indian-fighters, going on campaign meant marching into a wilderness that held too many opportunities for disaster. First there were the Indians, whose knowledge of the terrain gave them a marked strategic advantage. Then there was the terrain itself, ranging from the granite labyrinth of the Black Hills (*below*) to Southwestern deserts where the only water was often poisonous.

An early blizzard on the Plains might catch soldiers without heavy winter clothing. Rain could leave the trail a muddy quagmire. And the length of marches could destroy morale. In this harsh land, campaigning was often an endurance test — what a veteran called "a war of who could last the longest."

91

Troopers of the 6th U.S. Cavalry muster to ride out from their bivouac into Apache country in 1881. When such platoon-sized, lightly armed reconnaissance patrols encountered a numerically superior Indian war party, the tactic was, as one cavalryman put it, to "shoot and fall back—and it wouldn't have taken me long to fall back. I was scared."

TAKE CARE OF YOUR HEALTH.

The following extracts of advice to soldiers are from Dr. Hall and others:

1. In any ordinary campaign, sickness disables or destroys three times as many as the sword.

2. Sunstroke may be prevented by wearing a silk handkerchief in the crown of the hat, by a wet cloth, or by moistened green leaves or grass.

3. Never lie or sit down on the grass or bare earth for a moment; rather use your hat: a handkerchief, even, is a protection. The warmer you are, the greater need of precaution, as a damp vapor is immediately generated, to be absorbed by the clothing, and to cool you off too rapidly.

4. While marching, or on active duty, the more thirsty you are, the more essential is it to safety of life itself to rinse out the mouth two or three times, and *then* take a swallow of water at a time, with short intervals. A brave French general, on a forced march, fell dead on the instant by drinking largely of cold water, when snow was on the ground.

5. Abundant sleep is essential to bodily efficiency, and to that alertness of mind which is all-important in an engagement. Few things more certainly and more effectually prevent sound sleep than eating heartily after sundown, especially after a heavy march or desperate battle.

6. Nothing is more certain to secure endurance and capability of long-continued effort than the avoidance of everything as a drink except cold water (and coffee at breakfast). Drink as little as possible of even cold water. Experience teaches old soldiers that the less they drink on a march the better, and that they suffer less in the end by controlling the desire to drink, however urgent.

7. After any sort of exhausting effort, a cup of coffee or tea, hot or cold, is an admirable sustainer of the strength until nature begins to recover herself.

8. Never eat heartily just before a great undertaking, because the nervous power is irresistibly drawn to the stomach to manage the food eaten, thus draining off that supply which the brain and muscles so much need.

(51)

Where "a mistake meant disaster and disaster annihilation"

The regimental band played "The Girl I Left Behind Me," sentimental yet gay, and women's eyes were wet as the troops marched out on campaign. They marched with weapons slung, horses curried, wagons clean and tight, harness saddle-soaped to a gleaming black. Out of sight of the post they settled down to real travel, a snaking line of men and horses and wagons, moving in columns of four when the terrain permitted, or in a vulnerable single file that undulated for as much as a mile across rougher country.

Out here there was no band to play for them; the only sounds were the sounds of men on the march. Up and down the long line, cups and skillets hanging from the men's packs set up a tinny rattling against the thud of heavy brogans in march step, the creak of saddles and leather straps, the grinding of the wagons' iron tires, the gusty snorting of horses. There might be music of a sort, though. Sometimes, before things got bad and the men used all their strength in simply moving, a burst of song might float along the line as if carried by the wind.

But things got bad soon enough during a campaign. On a hard forced march men might move 60 miles a day under conditions that made life on the toughest post seem a pleasure. On the High Plains they slept in the snow, died of pneumonia or saw gangrened fingers and toes lopped off by Army surgeons. In the Southwest they traveled for days without water to drink. On one especially punishing march an officer reported that he "saw men who were very plucky sit down and cry like children because they could not hold out."

Along with sheer physical suffering in the field, the soldiers bore the psychological burden of knowing that they were on their own, usually far from any source of help. Colonel (and later General) Nelson Miles, one of the toughest and most vigorous officers in the Army, fully recognized the lonely perils of a far-ranging campaign. Once, describing a battle during the Sioux War of 1876-1877, he observed that every single man under his command "realized the desperate nature of this encounter, being then between three and four hundred miles from any railroad or settlement. Every officer and soldier knew that a mistake meant disaster, and disaster or defeat meant annihilation, and were therefore inspired to deeds of heroism and fortitude."

But simple fortitude and even heroism could not dispel the relative ignorance in which men on campaign lived and fought. The soldiers usually had little idea of exactly where they were going and, except in the smallest units, even less of what they were doing. The commander of an infantry company in a 20-week campaign, which ranged through Wyoming, Montana and Dakota, testified to this confusion in a sort of diary of life as he saw it. During the years of the Sioux conflict —the most extensive single Indian war in the history of the West—Captain Gerhard Luke Luhn wrote a series of affectionate letters to his wife, which she carefully saved. Luhn was an easygoing man of simple tastes. He worried about his children and often reassured his wife that he would take no unnecessary chances. His spelling, punctuation and grammar were matters of impulse and now and then scaled extraordinary heights of improvisation, but his very incoherence somehow lends authenticity to his account of battle. With bullets flying and orders constantly changing, he seems to say, a man might never know exactly what was happening at any given moment, but simply did his best.

"My dear wife," Luhn writes on June 19, 1876, from a temporary bivouac on the Tongue River. "We left this Camp 180 Infantry mounted on mules and all

Recruits got detailed—if somewhat dismaying—advice on campaign health care from *The Soldier's Handbook*, a pocket-sized volume issued late in the Indian wars.

the Cavelry 100 rounds per man and four days rations first day we marched 42 miles. next morning we left camp about 6 a.m. @ 8 A.M. the column was halted oweing to the scouts comming in and reporting having seen the Indians drive a heard of ponies, but the Indian scouts had not been in more then an hour when the crows spied the sioux near us and the fireing commenced, we had unsadled, Capt. Munsons company and mine the first out as skirmishers, Genl. Crook thought it would not amount to much thinking there were only a few hundred of them but he found out in a very few minutes that he had Mr. Sitting Bull *with* his entire band to fight. so that in a short time all the Infantry was out. but soon came back sadled our mules and went at a galop for about a mile deployed as skirmishers mounted and dismounted and went into the red skins the battle lasted about four hours when the [y] all of a sudden disapeared, and did not show themselves again, we lost in the Cavelry 9 men killed and about 20 wounded Cain had three men wounded two slightly and one man whom was shot by his own company will lose his leg my men did not get a scratch Corpl Ropen got a hole through his hat."

Captain Luhn's report of battle, like any other single account, presents only a partial picture, for a soldier of the Indian wars took to the field in many different situations. Sometimes, like Luhn, he was part of a small army of many companies and even regiments. More often he went out in a party of 15 to 60 men, led by a sergeant or a single officer, and rode hard in pursuit of an Indian band that had already struck its blow and was now slipping away. He might find an Indian trail in 12 hours and see action in 24, or he might ride for weeks without a sign of his enemy. Sometimes he was gone for months. The last entry of an 1876 diary kept by George S. Howard of the 2nd Cavalry reads: "Arrived at Fort Saunders" —probably Fort Sanders, Wyoming —"Nov. 5th after being out 8 months and 19 days and in the saddle 2600 miles, a pretty fair summer campaign." But however long a campaign lasted and however well it turned out in the end, a man never knew when he started just where he was going and what would happen when he got there.

Certainly a young cavalryman in Texas named James B. Gillett was the picture of ignorance one day in 1875. On that day, to his intense pleasure, he was cho-

Preparing for a march through Montana in 1876, skinners cinch flour barrels on a mule. Ornery but hardy, mules were used on long treks because they could carry 300 pounds for 24 hours without water.

sen to be one of 17 men who set out in pursuit of a band of 15 Apaches who had raided a ranch and were driving a herd of horses into the wastes of west Texas. Gillett was 18 and for some three months had been a member of the Frontier Battalion of the Texas Rangers, which then functioned as a state militia.

Years later he recaptured the bright days of his youth in a memoir. Though he came of an educated Texas family, the Civil War had left his father impoverished and Gillett soon found it both expedient and pleasing to drop out of school. He "substituted the wide open volume of nature" for books, became an expert fisherman and hunter and at 14 was selling his fish and game on the streets of Austin. During the next four years he hired on as a cowboy, made at least two trail drives, became a skilled horseman and decided to enlist. Soon he was mounted on a big black horse named Coley and counted himself a soldier. Now he would get his first taste of Indian fighting.

When a horseman who had ridden all night brought news of the raid, the company captain, Dan W. Roberts, decided to lead the pursuit himself. Gillett rolled

10 days' rations and 100 rounds of ammunition in his blanket and lashed the blanket to his saddle. He was also carrying a .50-caliber Sharps carbine in a saddle socket under his left knee, a .45 Colt revolver on his right hip and a 10-inch Bowie knife on his left hip. The order came—"Mount up!"—and the boy swung into his saddle, already tough but still untried, his heart racing with excitement.

Roberts knew the terrain well. He believed the Indians would move north of the San Saba River, then turn west, and he chose a route that would intersect their trail. After the troop forded the San Saba, Roberts placed his most capable scouts 400 yards ahead so they would be able to spot the trail before the troop obliterated it. Eventually they saw an old pony standing head down; Roberts guessed immediately that the animal had been abandoned by the fleeing Indians. He approached the worn old horse, which had been cut with a lance and had back sores, and at that point he found the Indians' trail, which was about 20 yards wide. Young Gillett noted that his captain "walked over the sign, scrutinizing every pony track, bunch of grass and fallen leaf." Blood and sweat had dried on the old horse and Roberts believed the Indians had passed through the area many hours earlier, about sunrise. They were moving fast; he reckoned that they were already 40 miles away. It would be a long chase.

That night the troop left the Indians' trail to camp at Kickapoo Springs, the only water nearby. They had come more than 60 miles, but they moved out again at daybreak. When they camped that noon, at a sinkhole, they had made another 30 miles—but now they ran into trouble. The horses stumbled into a rattlesnake bed and two of them, including Roberts', were bitten. Two soldiers were ordered to remain with the injured horses, to ride home if the horses lived and walk home if they died. As for Captain Roberts, he mounted a pack mule and continued the march at the head of his little troop, now numbering 15 men.

In the middle of the next day the signs indicated that the Indians had bunched their captured herd of horses and had remained in one place for some time. Roberts swept the horizon with his glasses and saw nothing. He walked a huge circle and soon found the trail of a single Indian who had moved away from the bunched herd on foot. He followed the tracks to a fallen live-oak tree and saw what had happened. The Indian, having come upon a herd of wild mustangs, had alerted his companions, then crept close and killed a big brown mare for meat. Roberts found both a shell from a .50-caliber buffalo gun and the horse itself, from which the Indians had cut the ribs and a hindquarter.

Roberts smiled. "Boys," he said, "we now have ninety-five chances out of a hundred to catch those Indians. They will not carry this raw meat long before stopping to cook some. We have followed now over one hundred and fifty miles, and they have never stopped to build a fire. They are tired and hungry and probably know where there is water not far away."

Gillett marveled at his captain's insight. They went on, past the last draw of the South Concho River and toward the Pecos. Here they came to a rocky mesa, pocked with water-filled depressions. From this point they could see 15 miles of their own back trail. It was obviously a perfect place for hunted men to stop; the Indians had made three fires, cooked the mustang ribs and picked them clean. The ashes were cold and Roberts thought the Indians had left early that morning. The troop followed until the trail, after leading due west for 200 miles, suddenly turned north. The Captain was puzzled. They followed slowly, cautiously. Within a mile they found a brushy place where the Indians had cooked more meat and here the fires were still live. Then the Indian track struck west again. It was clear now that the Indians were moving slowly and aimlessly, relaxed, well fed, feeling out of danger.

The soldiers camped that night without a fire—for its light might give them away—and marched again before dawn. After six miles they saw a tiny dust cloud ahead of them. Roberts studied it with his glasses and said it was the Indians. He ordered the men to dismount, place their extra gear on the ground, tighten their cinches and make ready to fight. "As we carried out this order," Gillett remembered, "a distressing stillness came over the men." Only Roberts and his sergeant had ever been in combat, and "I suppose the hearts of all of us green, unseasoned warriors beat a little more rapidly."

The Indians were on open prairie dotted with low clumps of mesquite and there was no way to move up to them without being detected. Roberts formed his men in a column of two and rode at a quick trot toward the Indians, trying to get as close as possible. They

97

A cavalry column snakes along a Kansas bluff trying to hold the standard four-abreast formation. If the troops dismounted when attacked, one man in each row would hold the horses while the other troopers fired.

were within 500 yards when the Indians discovered them. The Apaches galloped to a knoll, dismounted and, in a move unusual among warriors of the Old West, deployed in a formal fighting line. Roberts smiled. "Boys," he said, "they are going to fight us."

As a child, Jim Gillett had dreamed of fighting Indians. "At last I was up against the real thing," he wrote, "and with not so much as an umbrella behind which to hide. I was nervous. I was awfully nervous." But the moment to strike had come at last. A hundred paces from the Indian line Roberts ordered his men to dismount. Fire burst from both sides, and soldiers and Indians alike shrieked and yelled. Gillett saw two Indian horses fall and one warrior wounded. Immediately afterward the Indians took to their horses and scattered. Roberts shouted for his men to mount and chase them down. Excited by the gunfire, Gillett's black horse Coley whirled round and round while the rider's foot stabbed for the stirrup. When Gillett finally rose to his saddle he saw, directly before him, an Indian running on foot, Winchester in hand. Then a mounted Indian galloped up and the man on foot leaped up behind him. At once, Gillett gave the black horse its head. The Indians' horse was a good one, but the thought flashed through Gillett's mind "that no grass-fed pony on earth could carry two men and get away from me and old Coley." He began to close the gap, and the Indian with the Winchester fired at him, holding the gun in one hand. But Gillett's battle nerves had passed and now he was thinking coolly. He clamped his knees against Coley and fed cartridges into his Sharps, one at a time. He was close enough now to see that the warrior with the Winchester was old.

Over his shoulder Gillett saw his friend Ed Seiker coming up behind him. Seiker waved him on. When the Indian had emptied his rifle he drew his bow and fired arrows at Gillett, who continued to draw closer and closer. The Indians' horse swerved into a mesquite thicket and Gillett followed, snapping a shot that hit the horse in the head. It crashed to the ground, dead, in 20 feet, pinning its rider. The second man was thrown free and sprinted away through the mesquite. Gillett and Seiker chased after him. The Indian took shelter behind a tree, and Gillett's next shot burst bark six inches over his head. He ran again. This time Seiker's shot caught him square between the shoulders and killed

him. Standing over the fallen warrior, the two soldiers saw that he already had a bullet wound in his ankle, his bow had been splintered by another shot and there were only three arrows left in his quiver. Seiker scalped him. When they returned to the fallen horse they found that the pinned Indian had worked his way free and escaped. Soon afterward the soldiers recaptured the herd and, partly because their own supplies were almost exhausted, decided that the Indians had been sufficiently punished. They went home, Gillett tells us, "hungry and tired but highly elated over our success."

The very fact that it ended in clear-cut action set Gillett's brief campaign apart from most in the Old West. Many soldiers marched for months without seeing an Indian — and if they did meet in combat the encounter was likely to be frustratingly inconclusive: the Indians kept slipping away. Plains Indians were among the finest light cavalry in world history, and with rare exceptions the soldiers could not keep pace with them. The Indians, however, fought with their families nearby, and particularly in winter were crippled by problems of supply. They were constantly running out of rifles and bullets, food for their families and grass for their ponies. Soldiers had weapons that in the long run were stronger than guns — doggedness, discipline, singleness of purpose and constantly replenished supplies sent out by railroad and wagon. Across the West, soldiers pushed ahead and Indians retreated, but individual soldiers paid for these ultimate victories in the coin of physical suffering.

This suffering was not, of course, any part of the Army's intention for its men. According to its lights, the U.S. Army placed troops in the field who were more than adequately equipped and trained to endure the rigors of the longest campaign. An infantryman under heavy marching orders left his post with a 50-pound load on his back that generally contained, in addition to his rifle and 150 rounds of ammunition, half a pup tent (a two-man shelter tent), rations for several days, a blanket, a rubber sheet to be spread on the ground, and extra clothes and shoes. Cavalrymen carried the same supplies on their horses, plus 15 pounds of grain; their special armament consisted of a short-barreled carbine and often a saber.

Once in the field both infantry and cavalry soon settled into a routine designed for maximum efficiency and

100

Their canteens and mule-packed water barrels depleted in the 100° heat of a Montana summer, troops of the 22nd U.S. Infantry interrupt their maneuvers to break out shovels and dig around in the mud of a shallow stream bed in hopes of finding a usable trickle of spring water beneath.

even a small measure of comfort. The march itself, to begin with, was carefully planned to get the most out of men and animals without exhausting them. On the trail, the troops fell into formations that would remain essentially unchanged throughout the day. Ranging far in advance were hard-working pioneer details whose job it was to find or make passable trails for the men who followed them. Then came the main line of march, usually organized in a strict order of precedence: first cavalry, then infantry, then wheeled vehicles. Even within this order there were gradations. Senior officers took the lead; normally, no one in a column could ride ahead of them. Both the cavalry and the infantry were expected to form into columns of four wherever the terrain permitted. Among wheeled vehicles, artillery preceded supply trains, and bringing up the rear were light ambulance wagons for the lame, the sick and the wounded. Flank and rear guards took their places well outside the main column at the beginning of each day's march.

The march itself could be hellishly difficult, particularly because of the heavy supply wagons carrying food, water, tents and other gear. Although these wagons made long campaigns possible in the back country, they also created special kinds of hardships. Most marches were made over open terrain, since the Indians did not follow roads and neither did the soldiers who were chasing them. The wagons and the lighter "wagon guns" (as the Indians called cannon) thus had to be maneuvered through the roughest kind of ground. Pioneer details were often forced to cut crude roads through deep ravines, a job that kept them out of sight of the main column and vulnerable for hours. Going up mountains, whole companies tugged on long ropes to help the mules drag the creaking wagons. Getting them across rivers was not only difficult but also dangerous, especially when there was ice on the banks or the wa-

ATTENTION BATTALION!

DRAWERS, $8.   SHIRTS, $8.

Attention to Orders!

GENERAL ORDERS, No. —. I. The commander-in-chief having discovered the wonderful properties contained in the PERFORATED BUCKSKIN UNDERMENTS, patented by Colonel Hamilton E. Smith, as a cure and preventive of Rheumatism, besides being the greatest preserver of health ever presented to the Army, recommends their use to his subordinate officers and men for the following reasons:

They are indispensable to all suffering from colds,
They will prevent sudden cold;
They will positively cure Rheumatism;
They are indispensable whenever and wherever the wearer is exposed to the inclemency of the weather;
They keep the body in a uniform degree of heat;
They are patented and warranted;
They received the first premium and medal at the American Institute Fair of 1869;
They are recommended by the Medical fraternity.

II. With such an array of evidence in regard to the sterling qualities these garments possess, their use is generally recommended, and it is hoped the Army will adopt them whenever possible.

By order of ————

Manufactured and sold by

ANDRUS BROS. & ADAMS,
AMERICAN EXPRESS BUILDING,
55 to 61 HUDSON ST., New York.

ters were running at flood. In fact, crossing a river could be dangerous enough even without wagons. George Forsyth, the indomitable fighter of Beecher's Island, once led a marching column into a running stream and was bowled over, horse and all. His life was saved by a quick-thinking packmaster who managed to throw him a rope.

Whenever possible, commanders tried to pace a march so that their forces would not be overtaxed. Usually, a morning's march lasted no more than four or five hours. An hour or two before noon the column halted for a two-hour break, mostly for the benefit of the animals. Horses and mules were rested, fed and watered. The men, who rarely lit fires for the break, might take a cold midday meal of hardtack and salt pork. But the remainder of the day's march would be short. By midafternoon or soon thereafter the column would halt again and settle down to the complicated procedures of making camp, taking the big evening meal and bedding down for the night. The troops needed daylight hours for the chores that lay ahead.

As always, the animals came first: picket lines were set up for the horses and mules, and once again they were fed and watered. Then the men scattered to a variety of tasks. Each company began to settle into its assigned area, and guards were posted to the area's perimeter. Details went out for water and for fuel —wood when there was any, a substitute when there was not. One man, James D. Lockwood, remembered that when no wood was to be had "each soldier upon coming into camp after a day's march was expected to take a sack and go around over the prairie and collect it full of Buffalo Chips." On one march Gerhard Luhn brewed a cup of tea over a makeshift stove consisting of a buffalo skull with grass burning inside it.

In short order the little two-man pup tents went up. In big campaigns there would be large conical Sibley tents in which 10 or 15 men would sleep in a pattern like the spokes of a wagon wheel, with their feet toward the center pole or—luxury of luxuries—toward a wood-burning stove.

Above all, there was that evening meal, the big meal of the day. When it had been cooked and eaten, the men could settle down at last. Now was the time for poker-playing, letter-writing, diary-keeping and much talk under the stars—talk full of gossip, jokes and endless gripes about the officers, the campaign, the country, the universe. The sleep ahead might be peaceful—unless mules and horses stampeded or an Indian attack occurred or seemed imminent. But in any case the sleep would be short. Out in the field the men heard reveille before sunrise and were on the march again while it was still dark. Never did more than two hours elapse between the first bugle call and the resumption of the march, and on most marches even that time could be cut considerably.

Nothing in the Army's way of doing things was more impressive than the efficiency of this morning routine. During a four-month march in 1888, the 8th Cavalry broke camp and hit the trail day after day in exactly an hour and a quarter, between 4:45 and 6:00 a.m. Below is their high-pressure morning schedule—complete with bugle calls—as one of the men on that march recalled it, together with a brief log of their duties:

4:45 a.m. First Call! The men rolled out of their blankets and got moving;

4:55. Reveille and Stable Call! They came to order, saddled the horses and harnessed the mules;

5:00. Mess Call! They had half an hour to prepare and eat a meal, perhaps the most relaxed spell in their morning's routine;

5:30. General (Strike Camp)! The busiest time of all, when the troops struck tents and stored equipment;

5:45. Boots and Saddles! The cavalrymen mounted their horses;

5:55. Fall In! The entire column assembled in the line of march;

6:00. Forward March!

All of the prescribed campaign routines, inevitably, were predicated on an ideal march under ideal field conditions. In sober fact, marches were often made under conditions that fell far short of the Army's hypothetical supply tables and rules of procedure. Meals, for example, never a strong point in the 19th Century Army, deteriorated under field conditions from barely adequate to simply awful. Army supply wagons supporting the march were loaded with barrels of greasy salt pork and hardtack, plus dried beans, coffee and sugar. And for emergencies, a man was expected to carry another 10 pounds of salt pork and hardtack on his back—enough, according to the Army manuals, to last five days. According to the soldiers who had to eat the stuff, however, these iron rations were enough to kill a man in just about that same amount of time.

Fortunately, fresh meat was also issued now and then. The officers usually had no real objection to a bit of fishing and hunting when opportunity offered, though the rules of march promulgated by the generals back at headquarters forbade unauthorized shooting of any kind. Lucky campaigners might bring a few potatoes or onions from the post, or even pick up a pie or some biscuits from a farm woman along the route.

At mealtimes, the men set about building fires. And since there were no company cooks on the trail, each soldier was expected to apply his training in the culinary arts. He was issued a cleverly crafted mess kit consisting of a tin plate and a collapsible skillet—implements that many men promptly discarded in favor of a solid skillet and a big tin cup from the sutler's store. The food had to be cooked, for raw or half-raw rations were not safe to eat. "It is of vital importance to every soldier to know this useful art," said the government-issue *Soldier's Handbook.* "Disease and often death is the result of bad and illy prepared food."

The men did their best. They parboiled their salt pork when they could, then grilled it over a fire or fried it in their skillets. They roasted their green coffee beans in the same skillet or in a Dutch oven, pounded them to powder in a sack with the help of a stone or a rifle butt and boiled their brew in the cups they carried everywhere. In a pinch, the cups served as stewpots. Ami Mulford, a young trumpeter of the 7th Cavalry, recalled how he compounded in his cup "a fairly appetizing relish of pulverized hardtack, bacon and raisins, boiled in condensed milk." In the field, soldiers even concocted a primitive sort of pastry-like dessert by frying moistened hardtack in pork grease, and then sprinkling it with brown sugar. ("Not a bad meal," commented Private James Wilkinson of the 2nd Cavalry.) ◉

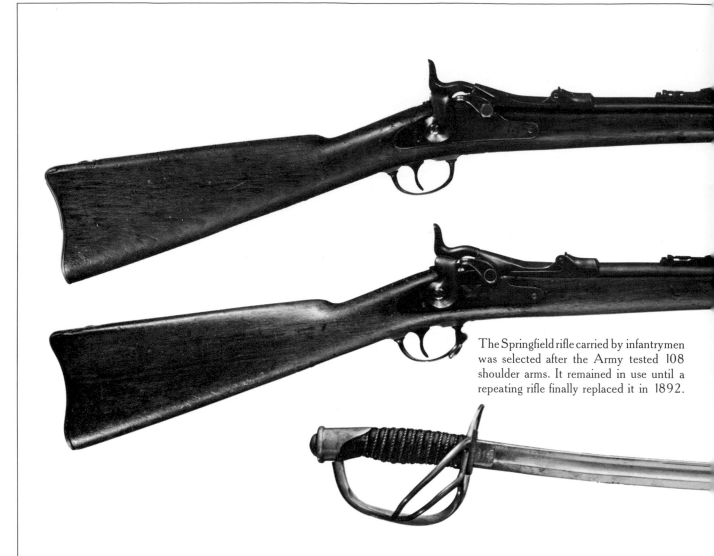

The Springfield rifle carried by infantrymen was selected after the Army tested 108 shoulder arms. It remained in use until a repeating rifle finally replaced it in 1892.

The lethal tools of the Indian-fighter

In 1873, the frontier forces received their first standardized arms issue. This belated action provided a boost to the fighting capabilities of Western soldiers by ending an impossible situation in which they had to make do with a chaotic diversity of small arms: repeating rifles, various kinds of handguns, plus some leftover Civil War weapons that had been converted to load through the breech—the back of the barrel—rather than the muzzle.

It was true that the saber issued to cavalrymen after 1873 was an 1860 model whose function was mainly ceremonial; and the light artillery (over-

leaf) did more to scare away the loosely organized bands of attacking warriors than it ever did to kill them. But the single-action Colt revolver and the new Springfield rifle and carbine—all employing .45-caliber ammunition—were first-rate arms.

The Springfields were single-shot breech-loading weapons. They could not be fired as rapidly as repeating shoulder arms like the seven-shot Spencers used by Major Forsyth's men at the battle of Beecher's Island in 1868. But they were less prone to misfires and had greater accuracy; their maximum range was 3,500

yards—at least twice the Spencer's.

Most soldiers and many civilian critics agreed with the campaigner who said "We could have been better armed." This opinion was based on the belief that a repeating arm would make up for their woefully poor marksmanship and give them a better crack at hitting their moving targets, but the Army stuck to these single-shot guns throughout the Indian wars. Aside from accuracy, the Springfield's range on many occasions kept Indians at such a distance that their muzzle-loaders, less powerful repeating weapons or bows and arrows were useless.

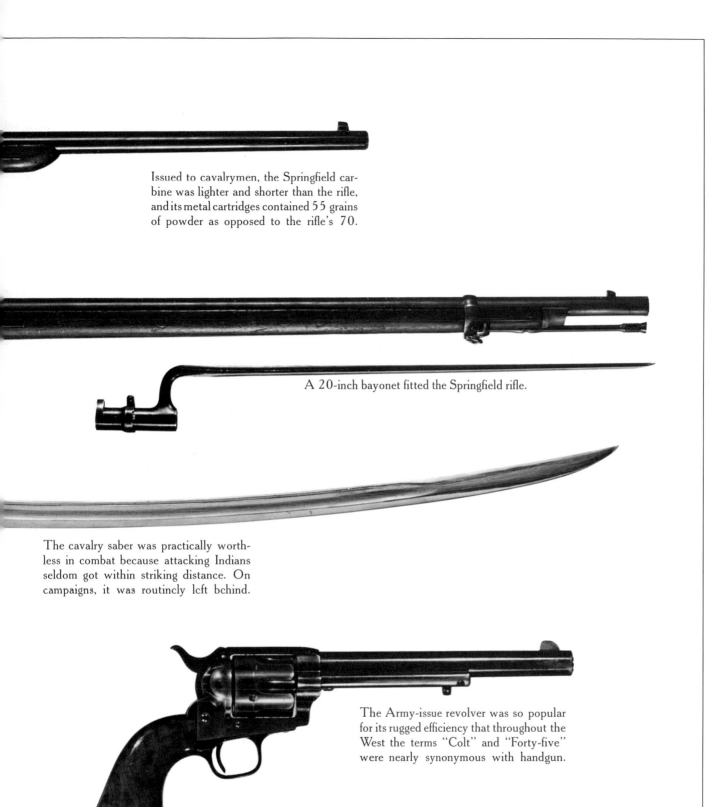

Issued to cavalrymen, the Springfield carbine was lighter and shorter than the rifle, and its metal cartridges contained 55 grains of powder as opposed to the rifle's 70.

A 20-inch bayonet fitted the Springfield rifle.

The cavalry saber was practically worthless in combat because attacking Indians seldom got within striking distance. On campaigns, it was routinely left behind.

The Army-issue revolver was so popular for its rugged efficiency that throughout the West the terms "Colt" and "Forty-five" were nearly synonymous with handgun.

The 10-barrel, crank-revolved Gatling gun could theoretically fire 400 shots a minute. But in practice, the barrels were easily fouled by the black-powder ammunition.

Most large columns on campaign hauled along a cannon that could throw two 12-pound shells a minute —although the aim of frontier artillerymen was ordinarily faulty.

But that was campaign food at its best—plentiful and reasonably varied. There were many forced marches on which men lived on half or quarter rations for days, marched 20 to 40 miles at a crack and fought engagements as they went. Sometimes they slaughtered their pack animals for food. On September 12, 1876, a column in General George Crook's Starvation March (pages 110-113) made 36 miles on a single meal of horsemeat, dried buffalo meat and a spoon and a half of beans per man. No rations at all were issued that night, and a diarist noted "men very weak and despondent, many unable to stand and some dropping unconscious without any covering of any kind."

Weather frequently compounded the miseries of soldiers on campaign. A recruit began to learn just how hard a march could be the first time it rained. He needed his half of a pup tent then, and was lucky if it kept him dry. Usually his blanket and clothes were soaked, and after a sleepless night he marched the next day still soggy. He may have grown used to it, or thought so—but the high incidence of rheumatism in the Army suggests that his body never did. Men sometimes went to sleep in wet blankets and awoke to find the blankets frozen to the ground. In cold weather they simply lived in their clothes. "I kept my rubber shoes on my feet for two months," wrote trooper John Larson of the 1st Cavalry, "and my socks kept my shoes company."

Writing his wife in 1876, Gerhard Luhn said that after one 180-mile march, "I inspected my mens stockings last night, and found 45 men out of 50 that had no stockings at all and the other five were full of holes." At one point he sent a blanket home, warning his wife that, like all of his blankets, it would be "totally spoiled full of grease, they have been used pritty rough, I have slept in them wet for several days in sucession I put on my Overcoat which would be dry and wrap myself up in either very wet or half dried blankets and through all this I have not felt a particle of rhumatism except four days, and two days newralogy."

In later years the Army made a real effort to supply effective cold-weather gear to soldiers like Larson and Luhn. By the 1880s the Quartermaster Department already was beginning to issue such items as long, woolly buffalo overcoats and muskrat caps. And General George Crook was ordering for his men a supply of ingenious arctic boots made by strapping buffalo fur overshoes around cork-soled Indian moccasins. In the field, however, much of this equipment still proved inadequate, and most veterans preferred to face the winter bundled up in their own personal gear. This was how one officer described his clothing during a winter march: "I am now wearing two flannel and a buckskin shirt, one pair of drawers, trousers of buckskin and a pair of army trousers, two pairs woolen socks, a pair of buffalo overshoes and big boots, a heavy pair of blanket leggings, a thick blouse and heavy overcoat, a heavy woolen cap that completely covers my head, face and neck except nose and eyes and still I am not happy."

Despite their attempts to keep warm, the winter cold often overwhelmed men. On one sub-zero day Colonel Nelson Miles observed: "That temperature is simply appalling. Even when the air was perfectly still and all the moisture of the atmosphere was frozen, the air was filled with frozen jets or little shining crystals." While marching through snow, horses and men regularly broke the surface crust, which slashed their legs until trails were marked in frozen blood. Lieutenant Frank Baldwin, of Miles's command, noted that "there was not a night that I did not visit my pickets every two hours, fearing they might freeze to death." Faces, ears, hands and feet froze as the men marched. Amputations were the frequent result.

Just how brutal cold weather could be was indicated in the diary kept in 1865 by Lewis Byram Hull, a trooper stationed at Fort Halleck, Wyoming:

Feb. 17—Snowed very hard all day. Chryst and Greaney lost; Greaney fell from his mule frozen so badly that he died during the night. Chryst stayed by him till morning.

Feb. 18—Chryst was found about ten miles from the post, badly frozen. Little hopes of his recovery.

Feb. 19—Warm and pleasant. Went hunting in the evening. Greaney found frozen solid, and taken to post.

Feb. 20—Arrived just as Greaney was being buried.

Mar. 2—Had a big time last night; made taffy. Sergt. Chryst died this morning.

Mar. 3—19 degrees below zero; ground frozen too hard to dig grave.

Mar. 5—No inspection. Helped lower the remains of Sergt. Chryst to their last resting place. No mail.

Yet men marched and fought in the worst weather the plains could supply. In January 1867 a young cav-

Their tents up and mounts unsaddled, Montana cavalrymen on a march in the 1880s fall to over a communal stew pail. The bottles contain condiments, like vinegar or ketchup, to spice dreary rations.

alry lieutenant named George A. Armes led 55 men to the relief of a party of woodchoppers who were surrounded in Dakota by Cheyenne Indians 40 miles away. Armes was an odd, contentious man who spent most of his life in a series of bitter battles with his superiors. At this point he was 22, and his vigor outweighed his intelligence or good judgment. He had been dispatched on patrol to recover some livestock taken by rustlers and was camped in a blizzard when a woodsman who had escaped the Indian siege found him.

Armes broke camp at 3 a.m. on a Tuesday in driving snow. At 8 a.m. he stopped for an hour, ate hastily, then moved on again. The snow was blinding. Men rode with their faces down, their eyes slitted, their hands tucked in their coats. Twenty miles farther on, a concealed mass of Indians burst from the woods with

shrieks and rifle fire, the noise of their attack partially muffled by the snow. Armes rallied his men and charged, driving the Indians over a ridge and into a ravine deep with snow. His horsemen floundered three miles up the ravine before he admitted that the Indians had escaped. One of his own men was missing, either killed or captured.

He gave his men time to brew coffee and take a hasty meal, then marched again for the woodchoppers' camp. The snow was a foot deep and drifting on level ground, as much as six feet deep in depressions. The soldiers reached the camp at 10 o'clock that night and drove the Indians away. The blizzard was increasing, the temperature falling. The soldiers warmed themselves at the woodsmen's fires, ate another quick meal and mounted again to attack the Indians in their village, 10 miles ahead. At 4 a.m. Wednesday they charged the village—and found it empty. But the Indians' trail was plain in the heavy snow, and the soldiers followed it for 10 more miles, sometimes struggling through drifts as much as 10 feet deep.

At noon on Wednesday Armes gave up the hopeless pursuit. He turned back, and between 11 and 12 o'clock that night the troop reached an isolated ranch. Armes was lifted off his horse. The ice on his face was so heavy that he could not speak. Only 10 of his 55 men were still functioning; he brought the remainder back in wagons, and most of these men lost toes and fingers. In 45 hours they had marched the appalling total of 125 miles, fought two actions, eaten three meals, rested hardly at all, and had never been out of the cold and the driving snow.

In the southern Plains and the Western deserts, heat and the shortage of drinkable water were almost as cruel on campaigning soldiers as the winter cold. Water could be chancy anywhere, of course; George Armstrong Custer, who fought most of his campaigns on the High Plains and in the Black Hills, once said that his troops could expect to find water every 15 miles—and then, in an afterthought, remembered that they often didn't. But the arid Southwest and Great Basin offered little water, and what water there was often made the men sick or killed them outright. Trumpeter Mulford spoke of "alkali bottoms where dust from the grass made breathing a torture and caused eyes to smart and swell." He noted that it was difficult to keep thirsty horses from drinking the alkaline water, which he described as "extremely repulsive in taste and smell."

Some streams ran so salty in the summer that their banks were crusted with white chemicals. It was miserable for men and animals alike to find such places at the end of long marches on which they had been sustained by the thought of water. Men drank stagnant water from buffalo wallows after skimming off the green scum that floated on the surface. Though they hopefully laced it with vinegar as a disinfectant, many sickened and some died. Old soldiers learned to conserve even the lukewarm dregs in their canteens, but recruits always suffered.

In August 1874 Colonel Miles marched south from Fort Dodge, Kansas, leading a supply train and more than 700 men in a campaign against the Kiowas. He started the march with a sizable pack of dogs, pets of the officers and men, but the heat was so unremitting that when they reached Camp Supply, about a hundred miles away, only two of the pack were still alive. One was Miles's own dog, a setter that had left the trail and sniffed around until he found a pool of water. A squad of soldiers who had collapsed on the march saw him return to the road, with water still dropping off him from his plunge. "Jack," they cried, "show us that water." Somehow Jack seemed to understand—or perhaps he simply wanted another drink for himself. In any event he did lead the parched men back to his pool—and by so doing probably saved their lives.

Sweeping the Kiowas before him, Miles moved on toward the Red River, heading into a belt of arid, broken country. His men and long wagon trains made a good 25 miles a day in the sun, hoping there would be water when they stopped. But, as Miles later wrote, "in many places no water was to be discovered in the beds of the streams, and only at long intervals were there found stagnant holes containing some, often impregnated with gypsum. Men rushed in frenzy and drank, only to find their thirst increased. The heat was almost unendurable, the thermometer ranging above 110 degrees in the shade, daily." For six more days they marched as hard as they were able, making 65 miles on the last two days. On the morning of the seventh day, near the Red River, they finally caught up with the Kiowas.

The Indians opened fire from positions on the bluffs and the soldiers charged. Captain A. R. Chaffee turned to his men and shouted what became one of the most famous lines of the Indian wars: "Forward! If any man is killed I will make him a corporal!" As the soldiers charged up the bluffs the Indians retreated in a running fight "for twenty miles over the roughest ground that I had ever seen men fight upon," Miles wrote. "Over the rugged hills and buttes and the jagged ravines and covers, and across the dry bed of the Red River which was now covered with white, drifting sand, through burning camps full of abandoned utensils, went the flying Indians. The sharp engagement and the long and rapid pursuit during the intolerable heat of sun and earth, and the absence of water, caused intense suffering among men and beasts." The Indians, too, were exhausted, yet they managed to keep ahead of the staggering soldiers. ◉

General Crook's Starvation March

Although Army expeditions against the Indians were hardly models of comfort, a miserable nadir on the campaign trail occurred on the so-called Starvation March led by General George Crook in the late summer and fall of 1876. Pursuing a well-mounted force of Sioux that had hit him hard in June at Rosebud Creek, Crook ordered his men to abandon all wagons, tents and extra clothes in the interest of speed.

Traveling light, Crook expected to catch the hostiles in the first few days of August. But the chase continued for weeks, through Wyoming into Montana and east to the Dakota Territory, without a battle. Fall came early, bringing hail, sleet and, at one dreary point, 11 straight days of rain.

By September 5 the Sioux trail had turned south into the Badlands. The soldiers' meager supplies dwindled, then ran out entirely. Famished soldiers wandered aimlessly off the trail; horses dropped to the mud as if shot and the troops fell to eating their exhausted mounts. "It seemed like cannibalism," one officer acknowledged later.

After five weeks Crook stumbled onto the Sioux at Slim Buttes. After a brief exchange of fire the Indians pulled back. By now the emaciated soldiers were in no shape to give chase, and they simply straggled south hoping for relief. On September 13 a supply train finally reached Crook. It took a month for the men to recuperate. Then as a last, face-saving gesture they disarmed Indians on reservations in the area.

Four of Crook's soldiers butcher a cavalry mount. During one week in September more than 500 horses were shot or abandoned.

A soldier wounded during the encounter at Slim Buttes jolts along Indian-style on a travois of lodgepoles dragged by a mule. Along level terrain the ride was tolerable, but on the rocky paths of the Black Hills a travois was agony for an injured man.

Looking more like squatters than soldiers, Crook's men prepare for another night on the muddy trail. With no tents, the best shelters the troops could fabricate against the unending rain were wickiups of branches, blankets and an occasional poncho.

Fresh troops from a relief train maneuver an ambulance through a pass in the Black Hills. In addition to the men wounded by Indians, many of Crook's soldiers were crippled by frostbite, scurvy and rheumatism.

Heading for an extended rest on French Creek, Crook's infantry marches past a civilian stockade built by gold miners in the Black Hills. Ironically the Army evicted the inhabitants just one year earlier because they were trespassing upon Indian lands.

Resting in the sun after the arrival of their relief, mule skinners lounge near a makeshift corral of mule packs. Lacking wagons, Crook's battalions had piled all supplies and extra ammunition onto mules, which characteristically showed more stamina than the horses during the exhausting march.

This supply train, camped on French Creek, brought some of the first real food Crook's men had enjoyed in weeks. Except for wild onions and berries scrounged along the trail, they had been eating the emaciated carcasses of their own horses and sometimes the meat of captured Indian ponies.

Nowhere along the Red River did Colonel Miles's parched troops find relief. "There was only found a small pool of saturated gypsum and alkali," Miles wrote afterward, "the stagnant water utterly unfit for use. During the chase the men suffered so greatly that some of them resorted to the extreme of opening the veins of their arms and moistening their parched and swollen lips with their own blood." The troops could not go on. The fleeing Kiowas made their escape —though Miles happily noted that "they had received their first lesson in our tenacity of purpose."

Miles's successful attack against a sizable body of warriors was an exception to the general rule of Indian-fighting. Even when they outnumbered soldiers, Indians disliked frontal assaults and massed defenses —not only because they lacked discipline, but also because they could not afford serious losses. Soldiers could call up new recruits, but Indians had no backup forces.

The Indians' guerrilla tactics, therefore, made sense, although some of their behavior in war confused soldiers. Indians delighted in a foray that demonstrated their personal bravery and fine horsemanship, even if the attack didn't accomplish much in any terms that soldiers understood. George Armes once wrote of a day on which a group of Indian warriors galloped madly all the way through a big Army encampment and out the other side while the soldiers fired some 500 shots at them, and no one was hurt on either side. Such feats baffled soldiers, but the Indians took great pleasure in them.

The Plains warriors were masters of decoys and ambushes, and soldiers often fell into them, partly because many of them held the Indians in contempt and partly because the nature of their campaigns called for chasing Indians no matter where they led. But experienced soldiers watched for ambushes and came to understand —sometimes after painful lessons —that the appearance of a few Indians just beyond rifle range was likely to mean that a great many more were hidden behind the next hill. Warriors who exposed themselves in this way to bait a trap were honored by their fellows for their bravery. What was more, they could expect rescue if they were hit, for Indians placed great store on recovering their dead and wounded for religious reasons.

On those few occasions when they did enter a pitched battle, the Indians preferred to gallop in a giant circle around the soldiers. Riding pell-mell over the

In an 1879 newspaper engraving, cavalrymen, besieged by Colorado Utes, shelter their wounded in a pit, and fire over a breastwork of dead horses and supplies. After a week, relief forces drove the Utes off.

roughest terrain, crouched low on their horses, they presented difficult targets as they attempted to shoot from their galloping mounts. If they were hit they could easily be rescued by their comrades. But fundamentally the cartwheel pattern of painted warriors whirling around pinned-down soldiers occurred only when the Indians outnumbered the white forces. On these occasions their circular deployment was the logical result.

The greatest asset that the Indians possessed was their intimate acquaintance with the country. They always knew where they were going, knew every water hole and canyon and bluff. War parties used this knowledge to elude the soldiers or to select terrain that would give them maximum strategic advantage in a fight. Simply following the Indians would have been all but impossible for the soldiers if they had not had the assistance of scouts. The best known of these scouts were mountain men like Jim Bridger or Kit Carson, who had spent most of their lives in this country. But friendly Indians were more commonly used—Indians who might be members of the very tribe the whites were fighting. Often the Army recruited such scouts by exploiting rivalries within a tribe. Sometimes it simply bought the services of renegade Indians and considered the money well spent, because hunting Indians usually

meant tracking them down, and tracking was an art that few white men acquired.

A cavalry officer, who watched Apache scouts study trails in Arizona, made a number of notes on their techniques. From a moccasin print they could determine the tribal branch to which a fleeing party of warriors belonged. From the discoloration of a patch of crushed grass they knew how old a trail was. The size of the trail revealed the number of men who had passed that way. The dryness of horse dung told them how long ago it had been dropped, and the kinds of grasses in the dung indicated the area from which the party had come. The position of urine puddles in relation to hoofprints showed the sex of the horses and, thus, the nature of the party. (Mares were most often ridden by women —and a war party would seldom use them.)

Homer Wheeler, a frontiersman and rancher who decided on impulse to become an Army officer and spent the next 36 years on duty, often marveled at the skill of Indian trackers. In his memoirs he gives an excellent description of the craft of a Cheyenne scout named Poor Elk, who joined a column of troops to intercept some Indians, presumably other Cheyennes, reported to have crossed the Yellowstone near Fort Keogh in 1874. The country had been overrun by buffalo and the grass

116

During an 1867 campaign in Kansas, Custer's 7th Cavalry came upon the skeletal remains of fellow cavalrymen who had been killed by Sioux and left, wrote Custer, with "20 to 50 arrows bristling in the bodies."

was cropped to the roots and trampled flat, yet Poor Elk spotted the trail at a point where half the command had already crossed it.

"Poor Elk followed about a mile to where the pursued party had camped. He brushed away the ashes from the dead fires and felt of the earth underneath, examined the droppings of the animals, counted the number of fires and noticed, by marks made by the pins, the size of the lodges; carefully scrutinized some moccasins, bits of cloth, etc. that had been thrown away; noticed that the moccasins were sewn with thread instead of sinew and were made as the Sioux made them; discovered that the calico was not as is used at the agencies, and found a bit of hair braid, such as Sioux Indians fasten to the scalp lock. A sweat-lodge had been built, indicating that they had remained in camp at least one day, and the droppings of the animals determined that the stay had been but one.

"The position of the camp, the tying of the animals near the tepees and the wickiups, the number of lodges, the care taken by the Indians in leaving, all these things furnished evidence as to the number of Indians and animals and the number of days since they had camped there. Though moving steadily, yet they were in no special hurry; were Sioux and not Cheyennes; had recently left an agency; had not crossed the Yellowstone at the time reported, but two days earlier; were evidently a party of Sioux who were on the way to join the Indians north of the British line. In fact, the record left by these Indians was as complete as though it had been carefully written out."

Sooner or later a fight would come, and white and red men would spill their blood on the land. The combat that fills the history books consisted of big battles, significant affairs in which many died and which shaped events that followed. But it was more often the little fights that illuminated the lives of those who were there —young cavalryman Jim Gillett riding down warriors who had stolen horses in Texas, Lieutenant George Armes struggling through a Dakota blizzard to lift a siege on a woodchoppers' camp, and numberless other instances of small groups of men showing coolness and daring under fire.

It took a man of special resourcefulness to survive these situations. When five cavalrymen were pinned down by Apaches in 1881, one of the men, a soldier named George Lloyd, emptied his rifle amid a hail of fire. In reloading, he accidentally slipped a .45 Colt's pistol cartridge into his .44 Winchester. Another soldier recorded that "it jammed, catching him in a serious

117

Indian scouts, along with an interpreter and an officer, crouch for battle in Arizona's desert country, where a 24-year campaign taught the Army the truth of the proverb "Only an Apache can catch an Apache."

predicament. However, taking his knife from his pocket, [he] removed the screw that held the side plates of his Winchester together, took off the plates, removed the offending cartridge, replaced the plates, tightened up the screw, reloaded his gun and began firing." Lloyd weathered the siege.

One of the most unusual and farseeing men ever to deal with the cunning Apaches was John C. Cremony. Originally a Boston newspaperman, he served as a member of the Boundary Commission that laid out the border between Mexico and the United States, and eventually became an officer in a regiment of California Volunteers. Cremony was decidedly an exception among the soldiers of the West, for he admired and liked the Apaches, though he regarded them as masters of treachery and never relaxed when he was around them. He may have been the first white man to know their language really well. In fact he produced a written compilation of the Apache language — a job he undertook on a commission from his commanding officer. From time to time, however, Apaches tried to kill him and, in return, he killed a number of them.

Once in Arizona, leading a party of 10 men, Cremony encountered a dusty place on the trail. As dust billowed around his companions, a band of Apaches fired on them from a distance of only 20 yards. None of the white men were hit, though several horses and mules went down. The Indians charged and Cremony emptied both his pistols at them. He had lost his long knife in the confusion and had no usable weapon left except for a four-inch dagger. Suddenly a powerful Apache appeared three feet away with a long knife in his hand. The Indian thrust at Cremony's chest, but Cremony seized his wrist and held it, and at the same moment lunged for the Indian's belly with his dagger. The Indian caught Cremony's wrist and the two men were locked together for perhaps two seconds.

Then Cremony tripped the Indian. As the warrior went down he pulled Cremony with him and rolled over him, snatching his wrist free. Bigger and stronger than Cremony, he held him tight, his knee on Cremony's left arm, his left hand holding Cremony's right wrist, his own knife poised. He grunted a few words that Cremony later translated as "white-eyed man, you will soon be dead." Cremony thought so too, though he observed later that "to be killed like a pig, by an

119

Apache, seemed pre-eminently dreadful and contumelious.'' The Indian's knife leaped for his throat. He jerked his head aside, and the blade went through his silk neckpiece and jammed in soft earth. Then Cremony seized the Indian's thumb in his teeth. The Apache tried to pull away but couldn't free his thumb. He howled with pain, and let go of Cremony's wrist to reach for his knife with his left hand. Instantly, Cremony stabbed the man with the short, sharp dagger, punching in between his ribs and killing him.

In another of John Cremony's brushes with death the hero was as much Cremony's horse as Cremony himself. The entire incident, which took place on one of the most desolate spots in the United States, testifies to the close relationship between a man and his mount fostered by long hours of grooming, feeding and drill.

In Cremony's day there was a 125-mile stretch between the New Mexican settlements of Doña Ana and Socorro without a single habitation. For 95 of those miles there was neither shade nor water. Worse yet was the imminent danger of attack by Apaches, who lurked in the surrounding hills. "They come sweeping down in more than usual numbers," Cremony knew, "and if successful in their attack invariably destroy all of the party for there is no possible chance of escape and the Apaches never take any prisoners but women and young children." Because of this threat, the stretch was known as the Jornada del Muerto—the Journey of Death—and Cremony made the trip alone.

He had a fine horse and he made the trip without difficulty. After spending two days in Socorro he started back toward Doña Ana at 3 o'clock in the morning. By mid-afternoon he had made about 55 miles; for half of them he had trotted on foot beside his horse in order to save its strength for any emergency that might arise. The sun "glared like a shield of red-hot brass," he later said, and he was thinking of stopping for a while when he saw a column of dust moving rapidly toward him from the left. To John Cremony that meant Apaches.

He halted and tightened his saddle girths, checked the four pistols he carried and fastened a folded blanket over his back with a buckskin thong. When he remounted, he saw the Indians galloping toward a point in the road lying well ahead of him. He spurred his own horse, and the big animal galloped at such speed that Cremony was 300 yards ahead when the Indians

reached the road. They turned in pursuit, but Cremony's horse was obviously faster than theirs. However, a full 70 miles lay between him and the nearest chance of assistance. He eased his horse a bit for the ride ahead and let the Indians draw within 50 yards. There were some 40 of them, armed with lances and bows. Fortunately for Cremony they had no firearms; otherwise, he would not have lived to tell the story.

As the Indians neared they drew their bows. An arrow struck Cremony's back, but it tangled in the folds of the heavy blanket and did not pierce his skin. He turned in his saddle and pointed one of his pistols at the Indians. At once they checked their mounts. At the same time he urged his horse on again until there were 600 clear yards behind him. Then he eased the horse again, and the Indians gradually narrowed the gap. Arrows grazed his arm and his thigh. He aimed his pistol, and his pursuers fell back. Then he rode ahead and again checked his horse until they drew near and arrows flew once more. Mile after mile they went, with Cremony nursing the great strength of his horse as he eked out the miles. The persistence of the pursuit surprised him until he realized that it was his magnificent horse the Indians were after—though they would, of course, have killed him in taking it.

By 8 p.m. it grew dark, but the sky was clear and the moon bright. Cremony galloped on. He came to a hilly section with the Indians 400 yards behind. Suddenly they disappeared. It occurred to him that they might know a shortcut through this hilly section. For the first time he spurred his horse to its topmost speed, and the gallant animal responded, bursting through the hills at a full gallop for nearly a quarter of an hour. Just as he reached the far edge of the rough stretch the Apaches struck the road again, only 80 yards behind him. When they found him still ahead they yelled with rage and resumed the chase, but now their horses were blown and weakening.

The pursued white man and pursuing Indians galloped on and on, with Cremony alternately speeding and easing his horse as he sensed its waxing or waning strength. At 11 p.m. he was within five miles of Doña Ana and, turning in his saddle, he started a steady stream of pistol fire that drove the Indians back and back. Finally, at midnight, he reached Doña Ana, "having made the distance of one hundred and twenty-five

A grim prognosis for the wounded soldier

"He who would become a surgeon should join the army and follow it," said the ancient Greek physician Hippocrates. Any young surgeon who joined the American Army during the Indian wars would have found the advice sound. Following frontier soldiers on campaign, surgeons received an education that could not be matched in the medical schools of their time.

One doctor, describing the curriculum, said, "The surgery was amputations for frost-bite, gunshot wounds, fractures and dislocations."

He and his fellows used instruments from a 17½-by-4-by-7-inch field surgery kit issued by the Army. The instruments themselves were superb, from the bone saw at top, fitted into the kit's lid, to the skull-piercing trepans at the bottom. But they were used under appalling conditions. Anesthetics and sterilization were rare to nonexistent in the hastily pitched field-hospital tents — or on the open ground of a battlefield.

The recovery chances for a wounded man amounted to less than 50 per cent. If a man was hit in the abdomen, his chances were close to zero; abdominal operations were so dangerous that surgeons hardly ever tried them. When such operations were performed, according to one account, surgeons would "hurriedly remove the evidence of the visit in the hope that the body would permit the insult to pass unnoticed." It seldom did.

Amputations were also performed quickly while the wounded man simply endured and then often expired. When Private Harry Eagan, Company C, 2nd Cavalry, was shot through

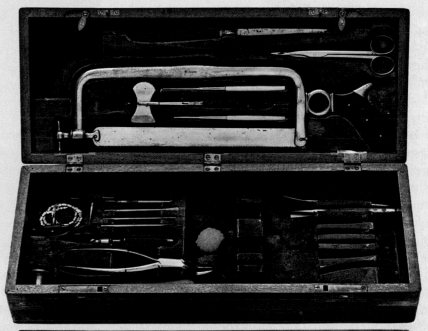

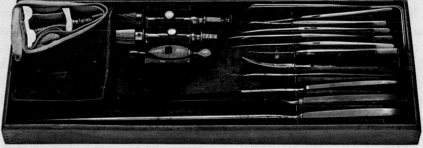

An 1870s surgeon's field kit held 47 instruments; a dozen have been lost from this one.

both hips by Nez Percé warriors in Idaho, an officer reported briefly and typically: "He died under the operation and was buried on the spot."

The worst cases were eye and head wounds, for which 19th Century surgeons in the field had no effective techniques. They simply prayed a wound would not become infected or clotted; and if it did they relieved the pressure on the soldier's brain by trepanning into his skull. Most times, instead of blood or pus, the brain itself would extrude through the hole.

For the men who managed to survive field operations, the ride back to base could be worse than the surgery: "I have had a case of fractured thigh," reported Dr. James Kimball in 1873. "We transported the patient about 350 miles and he is doing well." But a newspaperman on that trip remembered that the wounded man, in agony, begged Kimball to kill him.

The unknown heroes of the Indian campaigns

During the fierce decades of Indian-fighting after the Civil War, 416 soldiers won the Army's highest — and at the time only — decoration for personal bravery, the Medal of Honor *(below)*. During that period not one man above the rank of major earned the Medal. For example, the most famous Indian-fighter of them all, George Armstrong Custer, never did receive the award, though his brother Tom had won two in the Civil War and delighted in wearing them. (Custer, a consummate egotist, occasionally let his jealousy show; in a letter to his wife he noted that "Tom appeared at formal mess last evening wearing both of his baubles.")

The four recipients shown here were typically obscure fighting men whose bravery was recognized, and rewarded. They are pictured as they appeared in a turn-of-the-century chronicle, *Deeds of Valor*. Their portraits — taken many years after they had performed their heroic deeds and when those still in the Army had achieved higher rank — are surrounded by thematic ornamentations suggesting the nature of their actions.

PRIVATE JEREMIAH J. MURPHY
3rd U.S. Cavalry

A COURAGEOUS — AND LUCKY — FIGHTER

On a bitterly cold day in March of 1876, Jeremiah Murphy was part of a column attacking the village of the formidable Sioux chief, Crazy Horse. Murphy, detailed with five other men to form a picket line, suddenly found his tiny force cut off from the main column. One by one the men with him were cut down as they tried to fight through to the column.

Finally Murphy stood alone. But as he prepared to make a final run for it, one of his comrades, lying wounded, called to him: "O Murphy, for mercy's sake, do not leave me in their hands." The soldier turned back, hoisted the injured man onto his shoulders and tried to carry him to safety. Sioux bullets whined around them. The stock of Murphy's carbine was smashed by one slug — and then the wounded man took another round, this one mortal.

Reluctantly, Murphy put down his burden and set about trying to save himself. The main force watched in utter amazement as Murphy — now unarmed — raced back through the Indian warriors. When at last he reached the column, the border of his uniform was torn with bullet holes, but Murphy, astonishingly enough, was unscratched.

LIEUTENANT FRANK D. BALDWIN
5th U.S. Infantry

SERGEANT CHARLES L. THOMAS
11th Ohio Cavalry

SERGEANT MICHAEL McCARTHY
1st U.S. Cavalry

A GALLANT OFFICER TO THE RESCUE

One of only five soldiers in the history of the U.S. Army to be awarded two Medals of Honor, Lieutenant Frank Baldwin earned the first during the Civil War. The second came in combat against the Indians in 1874.

That year the Cheyennes raided heavily outside their reservation in the Indian Territory. In one attack during the summer they hit a family of emigrants, killing the father, mother and two elder children, and taking four younger girls captive.

A few months later Baldwin was leading a small force on a winter campaign in the Texas Panhandle. At daybreak on November 8, Lieutenant Baldwin's scouts rushed into his bivouac to report a large Cheyenne camp just ahead. It was the raiders.

Though vastly outnumbered, Baldwin launched a surprise attack. At first the startled warriors fled to a nearby hill. There, they wheeled about and charged. But Baldwin's troops routed the attack, captured the camp, and rescued two of the young girls. Subsequently, the Army kept up such heavy and sustained pressure on the Cheyennes that the entire band surrendered and set free their remaining captives.

A HARD-RIDING COURIER

In August 1865 the Powder River basin was swarming with Sioux. A column of 1,400 soldiers, part of a reconnaissance force sent out to quell the warriors, had not been heard from in 10 weeks. At headquarters near the Yellowstone River a call went up for volunteers to find the lost force.

The only man to step forward was Sergeant Charles L. Thomas. With two Pawnee scouts he rode out at 8:00 in the morning. At dawn the next day, they reached the Powder River — and the Sioux. Bands of Indians began to chase the trio. For hours, Thomas and the two Pawnees fought off pursuers.

At sundown, after 36 hours in the saddle, Thomas sighted the lost column. It was surrounded by Sioux, the men were scurvy-ridden and completely out of food, and not one officer knew which direction to take to safety.

Once inside their encampment, the sergeant used one of his 17 remaining bullets to shoot his pain-racked, exhausted horse. Then he mounted a fresh horse and rallied the demoralized men. They formed a fighting formation so strong that the Sioux gave way — and Thomas led them 150 miles down the Powder River to a supply camp.

A TOUGH MAN TO KILL

On a June day in 1877 two troops of the 1st Cavalry rode into an ambush in a canyon in Idaho. The attacking Nez Percés outnumbered the troopers eight to one. Moving fast, Sergeant Michael McCarthy with six men scrambled to a rocky elevation. From there McCarthy directed a barrage of carbine fire that slowed the Indians' advance.

Within minutes, however, the other troopers broke and ran, leaving McCarthy's little band to take the brunt of the attack. Rifle fire gave way to hand-to-hand combat. Somehow the seven men managed to mount up and fight their way through the enemy. Two of the men were cut down. When McCarthy's horse was killed, he mounted another. That horse, too, was shot. McCarthy, now separated from his men and out of ammunition, crawled into a nearby clump of bushes, while the other soldiers escaped.

When the battle was over, McCarthy saw Indians coming his way and realized his boots stuck out of the bush. It was too late to pull them back; he slipped out of them and crawled deeper into the bushes. At night he crept into the hills. Three days later, sore-footed but unhurt, he rejoined his company.

The stark vulnerability of a skirmish line at the height of battle is vividly portrayed in this work by Charles Schreyvogel.

Like shafts of lightning, the savage battles that shattered the monotony of a soldier's life in the Indian wars were hard to fix in the memory, even for the survivors. The re-creation of those violent moments called for the artistry of such painters as Frederic Remington and Charles Schreyvogel.

Schreyvogel's canvases capture the quintessence of battle on the Plains.

The fact is that he never saw an Indian fight; born in New York, Schreyvogel painted most of his major works on the rooftop of his home in Hoboken, New Jersey. To bridge the distance from Hoboken to the West, he drew upon a lifetime of exhaustive research. He was a fine horseman and crack shot, and had traveled extensively through the West, sketching and collecting Indian artifacts.

He combed archives and corresponded with old soldiers.

In tribute to his labors and art, *Leslie's Weekly* called him "the greatest living interpreter of the Old West," and defined his achievement in these words: "He has seized the significant thing out of the lives of the staunchest band of soldiers that we have produced yet, and has transferred that life to canvas."

Behind a falling trumpeter an unhorsed warrior runs for his life through the midst of a cavalry charge.

A beleaguered garrison defends its stockade. Attacks by massed warriors were rare but bloody.

Protecting a retreating column, two troopers make a stand in Schreyvogel's *Guarding the Cañon Pass*.

Ruthless leaders, battles without quarter

Every war in history has had a style, a dominating character all its own. During the long tragedy of America's Indian wars, all sorts of battles took place—foolish battles, battles well fought, ambushes laid and ambushes foiled, extended marches in which disease and weather took as great a toll as did bullets. But the common characteristic of these engagements was the total hatred with which they were undertaken and the intent of the antagonists to wipe out one another.

Three battles in particular demonstrate this terrible truth about the war for the West. They took place on a wide diversity of terrain—the mountain roads of Wyoming, the High Plains of Colorado, the deserts of Arizona. The odds for the antagonists were very different, and so were the objectives. The story on these pages describes the battles as the white man saw them. They were immediate and deadly in the eyes of the fighting troops but to the planners they were little more than the by-product of military strategy and long-range political goals. The Indian side of the story, told in other books, is simpler and more direct—the personal fight by men of a warrior culture for their ancestral hunting grounds. Yet in one respect at least the results were the same: merciless and systematic destruction of the enemy.

Of the three, the briefest and most disastrous for the whites took place outside Fort Phil Kearny, a post set up in the northern Rockies to guard a wagon road called the Bozeman Trail. The trail branched northwest from the Oregon Trail and passed through Wyoming, crossing the Powder and Tongue rivers and the Big Horn Mountains. It ended at the gold diggings in Virginia City, Montana. No one was overly concerned that the route violated a traditional Indian hunting ground, rich in buffalo, antelope and bear. Nor did the whites seem troubled that the Sioux under the tough, shrewd war chief Red Cloud had sworn to defend this territory and destroy the trail. Thus, with their usual ignorance of field conditions and disregard for Indian proprietorship, the generals in Washington ordered the soldiers of the Mountain District of the Department of the Platte to keep the road open.

The man who had to execute this order could hardly have been more poorly chosen. He was Colonel Henry Carrington, who in 1866 was sent in command of the 18th Infantry Regiment to build and garrison a series of posts along the trail. Formerly an Ohio lawyer with a sedate clientele of bankers, manufacturers and railroad corporations, Carrington had raised the 18th himself during the Civil War. But he had never fought with the regiment. Instead, he had proved so skillful an administrator that he was held to a series of staff jobs while other men took the 18th through its trials by fire. And its trials had been heavy: at the Battle of Murfreesboro, for instance, half its men were killed or wounded. Carrington's officers never let him forget that when his regiment was being tested, he was somewhere else.

In 1866 Carrington was 42 years old—a small, scholarly man who had chosen to devote the rest of his life to a military career and who still dreamed of fighting as a soldier in the field. As far as he was concerned, only poor health had blocked his ambition. A wiser man than he might have accepted his lot as a sign of providential guidance, for in truth Carrington could never have been an effective field officer. He was a handler of supplies, not of men. And Fort Phil Kearny, the key position in the line of posts he established on the Bozeman Trail, reflected both his virtues and his defects.

Carrington did an impressive job of planting the fort in unsettled territory under the constant harassment of

One of the best fighters to face the Army was Sioux Chief Red Cloud, who kept his vow to force U.S. troops off Indian hunting grounds in Wyoming and Montana.

135

Indians. The site was in many ways well chosen, near a source of water and on an elevation overlooking a good stretch of the Bozeman Trail. In building the fort, Carrington set up a timbering operation, erected a sawmill and laid out a complex as big as three football fields, surrounded by a high palisade and containing 30 buildings — among them a bandstand. The fort's only disadvantage was that it lay several miles from the nearest timber, and timber was badly needed — for constructing and maintaining the fort's 2,800-foot stockade and numerous buildings, and for fuel in the bitter Wyoming winter. Every day a small and vulnerable detachment called a wood train had to make an hourlong trip to the nearest forest and return. In a region filled with hostile Indians, the wood train naturally fell under constant attack. Day after day raiders would hit the woodsmen and their wagons; hastily the train would form into a defensive circle, and a rescue squadron would ride out from the fort.

In November, 33-year-old Captain William Fetterman joined the regiment. Unlike his commanding officer, Fetterman was a born fighting man. He had served with the 18th through the war, and he had been promoted on the field, mentioned in dispatches, bemedaled. He had emerged from the war with a taste for fire and an unshakable confidence in himself. This confidence was matched only by his contempt for Indians —enemies who struck and ran, who never faced up to battle, who refused to die in droves as white men had been doing back east. The idea that such savages could match disciplined regular troops struck him as ridiculous. And the cautious, basically defensive position that Colonel Carrington had assumed at Fort Phil Kearny struck him as craven.

Almost immediately after his arrival at the fort, Fetterman pointed out that the Indians were always free to strike the wood train, then flee unscathed ahead of the rescue squadron. In effect, he said, the Kearny garrison was virtually under siege. Blaming Carrington's lack of combat experience for the situation, and believing that the commander had been intimidated by the harassment of the wood trains, Fetterman argued for a punishing attack upon the Indians that would teach them a badly needed lesson.

The men at Kearny liked this line of talk, and Fetterman was soon leading a faction in the garrison against the commanding officer. One of his confidants was a young, hot-blooded cavalryman, Lieutenant George Grummond. Another was the regimental quartermaster, Captain Fred Brown, a balding, good-natured man who felt that he had been passed over for promotion and honors and was determined to make his mark against Indians. Several times Brown had pursued Indians recklessly, and they had fled. Like Fetterman, he was sure that the first really strong attack upon the Sioux warriors would rout them for good.

Besides being impetuous, William Fetterman was a braggart. The boast he made most often was that with 80 men he could cut through the entire Sioux Nation. Soon he was openly ridiculing Carrington — who had perhaps 300 men at his command — accusing him of timidity and even of cowardice. A strong commander would have stopped Fetterman, broken him in rank or even placed him under arrest. But Carrington temporized and in so doing lost a measure of control over his men. It could not have happened at a worse moment.

Only 50 miles from the fort the Sioux chief Red Cloud, Roman Nose of the Cheyenne and other war chiefs had mustered several thousand fighting men. On December 6 they attacked a wood train with a large party of warriors. Aroused by this unusually powerful thrust, Carrington sallied out in a clumsy counterattack and found himself briefly surrounded by a force whose numbers seemed to grow by the moment. He managed to get back to the fort with only two dead and five wounded. Carrington perceived that the Indian foray against the wood train had been only a feint, and he felt certain that even greater numbers of hostiles lurked nearby in potential ambush. Accordingly he forbade his officers to pursue fleeing Indians in any future battle.

Less than two weeks later, on December 19, Red Cloud struck again. Positioning some 2,000 warriors in hiding, he staged another decoy attack on the wood train — but this time Carrington made a cleaner escape. He sent out a relief detail under Captain James Powell, a dependable officer who drove off the decoys and refused to be lured into the trap. Next day Carrington put the wood train under an especially heavy guard and brought it safely home. He planned to do just one more day of timbering, then close down all outside operations for the winter. The Indians, of course, could not have known this. Yet by one of several coincidences that led to tragedy for the soldiers, Red Cloud chose that very day — December 21, 1866 — to stage the most elaborate and carefully planned of all his ambushes.

The war chief chose his terrain carefully. After passing Fort Kearny, the Bozeman Trail went past a ridge called the Sullivant Hills, skirted another called Lodge Trail Ridge, crossed over a rise and descended to a creek some five miles from the fort. On the flats along this creek, the Indians laid their ambush. Hundreds of warriors hid in the tall grass on each side of the trail; hundreds more waited on horses behind outcroppings of rock. And a fresh group of decoys was assigned to draw the soldiers over Lodge Trail Ridge, along the Bozeman road and into the trap.

December 21 was a clear, bitingly cold day, with the sun shining but a blizzard making in the distance. The wood train went out at 10 a.m.; at 11 a.m. it was attacked by Indians. As he had done two days before, Carrington ordered Captain Powell to take a relief detail to the rescue. But this time Fetterman demanded the right to lead the column on grounds that his commission was senior to Powell's. Fetterman's demand was absurd; moreover, he had been insubordinate for weeks. Yet Carrington, displaying his basic weakness as a commander, yielded.

Fetterman rounded up 76 men: 48 infantry armed with muzzle-loaders under his own direct command, and 27 cavalrymen with Spencer carbines under his subordinate, Lieutenant Grummond. Then the regimental armorer and next the enthusiastic quartermaster, Captain Brown, volunteered to mount up and come along. That made 78. Finally, just as the party prepared to leave the fort, two civilian employees of the Army, James Wheatley and Isaac Fisher, hurried up and begged to join the little force; their 16-shot Henry rifles made them welcome additions. Thus by a curious

coincidence — or by the strange fate that controlled his short, unhappy life — William Fetterman had exactly the 80 men he had always claimed he would need to smash the Sioux Nation.

Well aware that the outgoing column stripped him of his best fighting men and most of his serviceable horses, Carrington issued strong, unambiguous orders to Fetterman: "Relieve the wood train! Under no circumstances pursue the enemy beyond Lodge Trail Ridge!" And just before the column passed out of the stockade, the Colonel ran to the gate and repeated the crucial command: "Under no circumstances pursue the enemy beyond Lodge Trail Ridge!"

In later years Carrington often cited these orders in an effort to absolve himself of blame for what followed. But once he had turned a man like Fetterman loose, Carrington's subsequent orders came too late. The mistake had already been made.

Fetterman's infantry moved out before the cavalry was ready, marching boldly against the mounted Sioux warriors. The soldiers headed straight for Lodge Trail Ridge, but Carrington was at first not alarmed. They were as yet in no immediate danger, and if the Indians broke off the attack on the wood train, the soldiers would be in good position for pursuit. Abruptly, Carrington realized that neither the wood train nor Fetterman had marched with a surgeon. Quickly he ordered the assistant post doctor, a cool, fearless man named C. M. Hines, to check the wood train's casualties and, if no one in the train was badly hurt, to overtake Fetterman and return with him.

Soon after, as the marching column neared Lodge Trail Ridge, the Indians indeed broke off their attack on the wood train, fleeing before Fetterman's foot soldiers as Grummond hurried to catch up. These Indians were of course decoys, and so although they ran, they did not run very fast. In fact, their leader, a young Oglala Sioux named Crazy Horse, seemed almost to ignore the soldiers. Once the white men saw him dismount, apparently to examine his horse's hoofs and to adjust its bridle as bullets whined and chopped the dirt around him.

As the soldiers continued to advance, the decoys galloped off, paused, wheeled, rode back and forth. They behaved like men at play, taunting the white men, yipping like wolves. They turned and slapped their buttocks to show their contempt. Fetterman must have been infuriated. Was it possible that these Indians believed themselves safe, and thought the soldiers feared to follow them?

The decoys swept up the side of Lodge Trail Ridge and stood along its crest, yelling and gesturing. The infantrymen came behind them, well deployed, skirmishers out. The cavalry now arrived, passed through the infantrymen and reached the crest, just as the decoys faded over the other side toward the road. There, the decoys were met by a second party of warriors, who had been concealed near the fort and had swung around on Fetterman's left to join with Crazy Horse. At the same time the wood train's attackers had broken off and moved in on Fetterman's rear.

From this point on, the historical record is less clear. None of the white men survived the battle that followed, and Indian accounts of the fighting were not taken down until years later. But certain basic facts can be pieced together from evidence left on the field and from the Indians' hazy reports. Certainly, Fetterman did not obey his orders to stop at the ridge. He came to the crest, saw the taunting decoy warriors under Crazy Horse on the Bozeman Trail below and followed them down. When he reached the road he turned left, away from the fort, and continued along the trail, up the rise and down the other side. He must have been hurrying, for just past noon, only 45 minutes out of the fort, he was on the flats of the creek. The decoys went splashing across, their horses' feet breaking light ice.

The troops were now inside the Indian trap—Fetterman and his 80 men against 2,000 warriors. The cavalry, moving faster than the infantry, was out front and gradually drawing away. Thus, Fetterman's little force was divided as the trap was sprung.

When the decoys crossed the creek they, too, suddenly split again into two groups, then swung back toward each other. At this signal, an enormous force of Indians rose from the grass almost at the soldiers' feet, weapons at the ready. Suddenly all was confusion. Horsemen galloped into the open. Bows twanged, arrows skittered through the air and soldiers began to fall. Indian battle cries rang so loud in the cold air that the soldiers probably could not hear their officers. A mounted warrior charged madly into the soldiers and was shot off his horse. Grummond tried to rally the cavalry for a

stand. The two civilians and several soldiers who had joined them dismounted; in a moment they shot down several Indian ponies whose riders tried to rush them and used the ponies' bodies for barricades.

Fetterman started his infantry back up the slope they had just come down, struggling toward a shelter of boulders. Captain Brown let his horse run free and joined them. The cavalrymen swung up the hill to the left, perhaps in panic, perhaps trying to cover the infantry. Grummond died on the road, saber in hand.

Meanwhile, the infantrymen reached the rocks and began firing, their ramrods flashing after each slow volley as the Indians crept closer. Above them the leaderless cavalrymen milled on the slope, hardly firing their carbines. Eventually the cavalry reached the crest of the rise, but found no escape there. Indians were swarming up toward them on the other side. They dismounted, freed their horses and took whatever cover they could.

Far below, still on the road, the two civilians and the soldiers who chanced to be with them maintained a devastating fire. The civilians' 16-shot Henrys must have been particularly effective; frozen gouts of blood found later around the little group indicated that they had hit at least 60 Indians. But their ammunition soon gave out and the Indians overran them. They tried to fight on with knives, bayonets and gunstocks but in moments they were dead.

Fetterman's infantrymen lasted 15 to 20 minutes. As their ammunition dwindled to a round or two per man they bunched closer together. The surrounding Indians were so close that some arrows overshot and killed warriors on opposite sides of the embattled troops. Then, all at once, the Indians leaped over the rocks and dashed among the soldiers with lances and war clubs. As they came, Fetterman and Brown stood up, face to face, with their pistols at each other's temples. The two men must have counted down and fired simultaneously, killing each other and leaving clear evidence of their act by the positions of their bodies and the powder burns on their temples. At the very end of this phase of the battle, a few infantrymen broke out and ran upslope toward the cavalry. The Indians easily killed most of them in the open.

By this time Colonel Carrington, five miles away at Fort Kearny, knew things had gone wrong. He had heard the first blast of gunfire shortly before noon, and

The events that led to the ambush of Captain William Fetterman and 80 men in 1866 centered around Fort Phil Kearny *(right)*, on a mining road called the Bozeman Trail. To get firewood, foraging parties had to range miles from the fort. The map below, drawn 38 years later by the fort commander, Colonel Henry Carrington, shows what happened when one so-called wood train was attacked by Indians. First the train formed a defensive "corral" *(center)* just south of Sullivant Hill. Ordered to the rescue, Fetterman instead dashed north of Sullivant, after Indian decoys. At this point Carrington's memory erred: Fetterman and his men went over Lodge Trail Ridge rather than skirting it as on the map. But their fate is correctly indicated by the letters A, B and C, marking the spots where they fell.

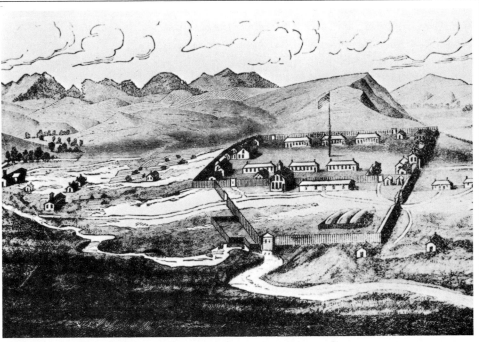

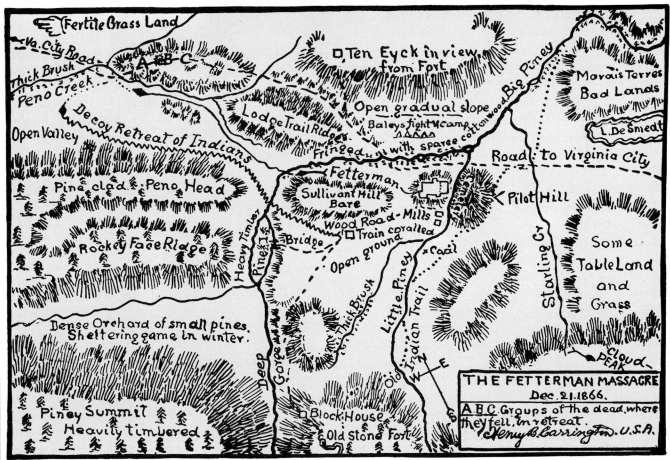

Fertile Grass Land

Va. City Road

Thick Brush

Peno Creek

A B C

Ten Eyck in view from Fort

Decoy Retreat of Indians

Open Valley

Lodge Trail Ridges

Open gradual slope

Baileys fight camp

Fringed with sparce cottonwood Big Piney

Marais Terres Bad Lands

L. De Smedt

Road to Virginia City

Pine clad Peno Head

Fetterman

Sullivant Hill Bare

Pilot Hill

Rockey Face Ridge

Heavy Timber

Little Piney

Wood Road - Mills

Bridge

Train corraled

Open ground

Starling Cr

Some Table Land and Grass

Dense Orchard of small pines. Sheltering game in winter.

Deep Gorge

Thick Brush

Little Piney

Old Indian Trail

Coal

N
W   E
S

Cloud PEAK

Piney Summit
Heavily timbered

Block House

Old Stone Fort

THE FETTERMAN MASSACRE
Dec. 21. 1866.
A.B.C. Groups of the dead, where they fell, in retreat.
Henry B. Carrington U.S.A.

immediately ordered a 75-man relief force of cavalry and wagons to prepare to move out under the command of Captain Tenedor Ten Eyck. Moments before, Dr. Hines, who had indeed left the wood train to find Fetterman, galloped back to the fort with inconclusive but ominous news. Hines had gone to a rise on the ground several miles from the fort. He had seen hundreds of milling Indians but no sign of soldiers. Ten Eyck's relief force marched at once, immediately reinforced by an additional 40 men—almost the last fighting men left in the fort's depleted garrison.

With his usual prudence, Carrington ordered Ten Eyck not to follow the fatal route taken by Fetterman. Instead, the captain was to march his men along a detour that led north from the fort, intersected the Bozeman Trail, and ended on high ground a full three miles east of the battlefield (map, page 139). From that vantage point he could survey the action and move to Fetterman's aid, if aid was still possible. If it was not, he and his men could beat a safe retreat to the fort. The fact was that by the time they left the fort Fetterman's infantrymen were dead, and the little band of cavalrymen strung out along the ridge was doomed.

On that narrow ridge—only 40 feet wide at the top, swept by cold wind and spotted with ice patches—the cavalrymen hunkered among the rocks. The Indians below paused to capture the freed cavalry horses, then returned to the attack. The position was considerably better than the one the infantrymen had found, and the cavalrymen might have held on—if only there had been more of them. But the huge force of Indians was determined to take the soldiers in a single decisive drive.

As the white men watched, the warriors darted into the rocks, leaping up, running, dropping for an instant, then dashing for the next bit of cover against the flaming carbines. Their advance was costly: cavalry killed many more men than the infantry had done below. But the Indians drove into the rocks until they could literally smash the soldiers down with clubs. A bugler beat them off with his bugle until it was battered shapeless. Then he lay with the others, killed by a dozen wounds.

From beginning to end the entire action had taken no more than 40 minutes. After the fighting the Indians moved about the field killing any soldiers who still lived. Then they stripped and mutilated the stiffening bodies as a double form of vengeance, so that the dead men's

An engraving of the Fetterman battle that ran in *Harper's Weekly* three months after the event shows most of the Indians naked to the waist. Actually, since the day was very cold, they had worn blankets.

spirits would be both helpless and disfigured. To blind the spirits they tore out the white men's eyes and laid them on rocks. They cut off noses and ears, chopped off chins, bashed out teeth, tore out entrails and laid them all on rocks beside the bodies. They cut off fingers, hands, feet, took arms out of sockets, scooped out brains. They split skulls up and down and across. They cut out muscles of calves, thighs, stomachs, breasts, arms, cheeks. Suddenly a soldier's dog ran from the rocks where it had been cowering. "All are dead but the dog," cried an Indian. "Let him carry the news to the fort." Another man drove an arrow through the dog. "No," he said, "do not let even a dog get away."

Their killing over and done, the Indians set about retrieving unbroken arrows — perhaps as many as 40,000 arrows had been loosed in those 40 minutes — and gathering up their own 60 dead and 300 wounded (of whom about 100 would die). Then they launched into a victory dance, just as Captain Ten Eyck's relief force drew up on an overlooking ridge. On the way out from the fort Ten Eyck and his men had heard gunfire to the west, but by the time he reached the high ground the sound had ceased. In the distance he could just make out a few stripped and mutilated bodies lying on the ground. But most of the dead were obscured by a shifting veil of Indians, over 2,000 of them, leaping and whirling in their celebration of triumph.

When the dancing Indians caught sight of the little relief force standing motionless on a ridge three miles away, they exulted all the more. Some of them taunted the white men, daring them to come down into the valley and fight. But Ten Eyck did not take the challenge: the dead were beyond rescue, and the odds were overwhelming. Moreover, he could see that the Indians were already beginning to move away westward, out of the valley. There would be no more fighting that day. Through the whole of the long afternoon Ten Eyck waited, holding his position. Finally, when the valley was clear, the soldiers went down to collect the dead. They did not have enough wagons for all, but they did manage to take more than half of the naked, torn bodies back to Fort Phil Kearny.

The fort itself was in a state of near-panic — and with good reason. With Fetterman's force slaughtered and Ten Eyck's men off on the relief mission, the post had been wide open to attack. Even now a sustained defense against an onslaught by the full Indian force would have been virtually impossible. That night, therefore, Carrington sent off a frantic message to General Philip St. George Cooke, his superior in Omaha. It began: "Do send me reinforcements forthwith. Expedition now with my force is impossible. I have had today a fight unexampled in Indian warfare." And it ended: "Promptness is the vital thing. The Indians are desperate; I spare none, and they spare none."

Once he had delivered himself of that anguished plea, Carrington acted with notable self-possession and coolness. He ordered that the women and children be placed in the powder magazine if an attack began, and arranged the powder stores so that he himself could explode it all with a single match. He even foresaw the possibility that he might not be there to do the job, and wrote down these instructions: "If, in my absence, Indians in overwhelming numbers attack, put the women and children in the magazine and, in the event of a last desperate struggle, destroy all together, rather than have any captured alive."

Finally he saw to it that an expedition was organized to bring in the bodies still remaining on the Bozeman Trail. Every enlisted man fit for duty volunteered for the assignment. A few officers raised objections, pointing out that a small party would not be safe outside the stockade, while a large one would leave the fort completely undefended. To these officers Carrington said: "I will not let the Indians entertain the conviction that the dead cannot and will not be rescued. If we cannot rescue our dead, as the Indians always do at whatever risk, how can you send details out for any purpose?"

Then Carrington settled down to wait. Aware of his vulnerability, he assumed that an attack was coming and that the Indians would almost certainly take the fort. But he forgot, or did not realize, that the Indian's tactics were nothing like the white man's. The thought of besieging or attacking the fort apparently never occurred to Red Cloud and his warriors. They had punished the soldiers. A blizzard was coming up, and it was time to move their families into winter quarters. They rode away well satisfied, leaving Fort Phil Kearny to nurse its grievous wounds.

But Henry Carrington had not met the last of his humiliations. A few days later General Cooke summarily relieved him of his command and sent him to sit out the rest of Red Cloud's war at a quiet, desolate fort in central Nebraska. (Meanwhile the foolhardy Fetterman was acclaimed a hero.) Eventually, Chief of Staff William Tecumseh Sherman reviewed the reports of the battle and remarked that "Colonel Carrington's report was fully sustained."

The Fetterman incident stunned the country. For the first time the question was raised whether the Bozeman Trail was worth defending—particularly when a new railroad then abuilding would soon make the wagon road obsolete anyway. Within a year, a peace commission agreed to close the trail if Red Cloud would let the railroad go through unharassed on a route curving far to the south. On July 31, 1868, less than two years after Fetterman's band of 80 died, all remaining troops were pulled out and the triumphant Sioux rode into Fort Kearny and burned it to the ground.

In time the tragedy on the Bozeman Trail came to be called the "Fetterman Massacre." In reality it was a battle—albeit a fatally foolish one—sought by Indians and soldiers alike, and won by the Indians.

The fact is that the Indian wars abounded in true massacres—engagements in which one side attacked an unprepared and sometimes unarmed enemy. To many white historians—and perhaps to Indians as well—the most heinous of these was the treacherous slaughter that Colonel John M. Chivington's Colorado troops committed on Chief Black Kettle's people at Sand Creek, in Colorado.

John Chivington was a Methodist minister from Ohio who settled in Denver in 1860, when he was 39. He became a presiding elder of the Rocky Mountain Methodist District, ran a church, organized a Sunday school and began circuit preaching through the mining towns. Chivington was an imposing man, six and a half feet tall, 250 pounds and barrel chested. He had a powerful effect on those around him, and he must have seen himself as destined for something more dramatic than the cloth. One associate later described him as "a crazy preacher who thinks he is Napoleon Bonaparte."

When Colorado raised a cavalry troop called the 1st Regiment for service in the Civil War, Chivington was offered a chaplain's commission. He refused, demanding a "fighting" rather than a "praying" commission. This view of himself as more soldier than solacer was sec-

onded by his own circle of admirers, one of whom called Chivington "the most perfect figure of a man I ever saw in uniform." And in fact, when Union troops were ordered out to stop a Confederate thrust into New Mexico in 1862, Chivington led the principal charge that broke the Southerners. He returned to Denver a hero. When the 1st Regiment's colonel resigned, Chivington took his place. "I believe I could run an empire," he once exclaimed to a friend.

In his drive for that empire, Chivington began making the regiment a platform for politics. With the arrival of John Evans as territorial governor in 1862, a movement began for Colorado statehood with Evans as Governor and Chivington as a Congressman. His future now depended on backing Evans and remaining a popular military and political figure.

Fighting an Indian war would give him an opportunity to shine in both spheres and he soon got himself made military commander of the District of Colorado. As miners and ranchers were drawn to Chivington's fief, Indian troubles mounted. Whites had made the usual effort to confine the tribes to ever-smaller reservations, but most Indians continued to hunt wherever they pleased. Their clashes with whites became increasingly serious. Settlers and miners demanded protection from their government—or better yet, the extermination of Colorado's Indian population.

Chivington's Colorado troops were sent out to punish the warrior tribes. With a combination of cruelty and stupidity, they attacked unoffending Indians, who counterattacked in retaliation. For Governor Evans the situation provided an opportunity for some old-fashioned demagoguery. "I am now satisfied," he wrote in a letter to the Commissioner of Indian Affairs, "that the tribes of the plains are nearly all combined in this terrible war. It will be the largest Indian war this country ever had, extending from Texas to the British lines."

To Secretary of War Edward Stanton he telegraphed with inflammatory inaccuracy: "The alliance of Indians on the plains is now undoubted. A large force, say 10,000 troops, will be necessary to defend the lines and put down hostilities. Unless they can be sent at once we will be cut off and destroyed."

They could not be sent at once, and Evans knew it. The Army of 1864, in the throes of a great Civil War, had nothing like that number of men to commit to

Proclamation

Having sent special messengers to the Indians of the plains directing the friendly to rendezvous at Fort Lyon, Larned, Larimie and Camp Collins for safety and protection, warning them that all hostile Indians would be pursued and destroyed, and the last of said messengers having now returned, and the evidence being conclusive that most of the Indian tribes of the plains are at war and hostile to the whites, and having to the utmost of my ability endeavored to induce all the Indians of the plains to come to said places of rendezvous promising them subsistence and protection which with a few exceptions they have refused to do.

Now therefore I, John Evans, Governor of Colorado Territory do issue this my proclamation, authorizing all Citizens of Colorado, either individually or in such parties as they may organize, to go in pursuit of all hostile Indians on the plains, Scrupulously avoiding those who have responded to my call to rendezvous at the points indicated, also to kill and destroy as enemies to the Country wherever they may be found all such hostile Indians, And further, as the only reward I am authorized to offer for such services, I hereby empower such Citizens or parties of Citizens to take Captive and hold to their own private use and benefit all the property of such hostile Indians that they may Capture and to receive for all stolen property recovered from said Indians such reward as may be deemed proper and just therefor.

I further offer to all such parties as will organize under the Militia law of the Territory for the purpose, to furnish them arms and ammunition, and to present their accounts for pay as regular soldiers for themselves, their horses, their subsistence and transportation to Congress, under the assurance of the Department Commander that they will be paid.

The Conflict is upon us, and all good Citizens are called upon to do their duty for the defense of their homes and families

In testimony whereof I have hereunto set my hand and caused the great seal of the Territory of Colorado to be affixed this 11th day of August A.D. 1864.

By the Governor

Jno Evans

S. H. Elbert, Secretary of Colorado Territory.

A desire to kill seethed within Colonel John M. Chivington, commander of troops at the Sand Creek Massacre. Preparing for that expedition, he exclaimed, "Damn any man who is in sympathy with an Indian!"

a remote sector of the West. Chivington's own 1st Regiment had been chasing Indians all summer and was clearly not up to the job. The 2nd, which had been raised soon after the war began, was campaigning in Kansas against the Confederates. Under these circumstances Governor Evans shifted his ground; he now demanded authorization to raise a volunteer regiment to be called the 3rd, paid by the government (Chivington would have overall command) and enlisted to serve for a limited period of time. Together with the 1st Regiment, these short-term volunteers—theoretically, at least—would provide an adequate force. "Otherwise," warned the Governor, "we are helpless."

Reluctantly, the Army agreed to let him raise a regiment for an enlistment of 100 days, thus accepting a makeshift solution to a constant problem. In other years, out of expediency, the Army had resorted to this solution to the need for short-term soldiers, and volunteers had come to play a prominent part in the Army of the West. Though some served with distinction, others —most notably Chivington's 3rd—turned out to be far more trouble than they were worth.

To begin with, raising a regiment of this kind was not easy. Steady, reliable men did not tend to rush off on 100-day adventures. However, Governor Evans did his hard-selling best to arouse the citizens. He plastered Denver with posters (page 146). He organized recruitment meetings at which high-blown oratory filled the air. To heighten the aura of urgency he declared martial law and closed all the saloons and most of the stores. Grocers and butchers were permitted to do business for a scant three hours a day. While he was at it, he forbade emigrant wagon trains to leave the territory.

It all worked—after a fashion. Before the end of August, Evans had his regiment of volunteers—the sorriest

An ominous prelude to the Sand Creek Massacre, this proclamation by Governor John Evans authorized Coloradans to destroy any hostile Indians they could find.

collection of flophouse scoundrels, street toughs, claim jumpers and assorted riffraff ever to put on the blue uniform of the United States Army. The process of equipping the outfit enriched many go-getting Denver merchants who busily scrounged government contracts.

Then a wholly unforeseen difficulty arose. Having been given his regiment, Evans came under immediate pressure to use it before the volunteers' 100-day term of enlistment ran out. And as it happened, the late summer and fall of 1864 turned out to be a most unfortunate moment to put an Indian-fighting regiment—especially this disorderly crew—into the field.

By the fall of that year, with the big prewinter buffalo hunts coming on, the local Cheyenne and Arapaho Indians were behaving more peacefully than they had in some months. Furthermore, the tribes were becoming more and more attentive to the mollifying persuasions of Chief Black Kettle, a Cheyenne leader who had argued consistently for peace because he thought the whites too numerous to resist. Black Kettle had even gone to Washington to meet President Lincoln and had been given a huge American flag, of which he was very proud. For a time during the summer Black Kettle's influence had waned as fighting fever gripped the warriors, but now his authority was rising again.

On June 27 Governor Evans had offered the tribes what appeared to be an amnesty. He issued a proclamation saying that Indians who did not wish to be killed could put themselves under Army protection. But he then issued a second proclamation, which invited white settlers in so many words to murder Indians and seize their property. Claiming that "most of the Indian tribes of the plains are at war and hostile to the whites," this second manifesto authorized "all citizens of Colorado . . . to kill and destroy . . . all such hostile Indians and hold all the property of said hostile Indians."

Yet the second proclamation did not quite cancel out the first one, for by using the word "most" it technically applied only to Indians construed as being at war. Unaware of such ambiguities, Black Kettle and

Of the 700 men in the Colorado Volunteer regiments that carried out the Sand Creek Massacre, many were recruited by hard-sell posters like the one below, with its tempting promise of the right to plunder.

ATTENTION!
INDIAN
FIGHTERS

Having been authorized by the Governor to raise a Company of 100 day

U. S. VOL CAVALRY!

For immediate service against hostile Indians. I call upon all who wish to engage in such service to call at my office and enroll their names immediately.

Pay and Rations the same as other U. S. Volunteer Cavalry.

Parties furnishing their own horses will receive 40c per day, and rations for the same, while in the service.

The Company will also be entitled to all horses and other plunder taken from the Indians.

Office first door East of Recorder's Office.

HAL. SAYR.

Central City, Aug. 13, '64.

several other chiefs took Evans up on his original offer of amnesty. Evans and Chivington were surprised and discomfited by this further slackening of hostilities; but they grudgingly promised that the Indians would not be molested if they reported to Fort Lyon in eastern Colorado and stayed there. Black Kettle agreed and the Indians set off for the fort. At this point a chance order by the commandant of Fort Lyon played directly into the hands of the war-minded officials, who desperately needed an excuse for a fight. When the Indians reported in, they were instructed to camp about 40 miles away, on Sand Creek. Thus they were not literally at the fort, as the agreement with Evans said they should be.

The month was now November 1864. The 3rd Colorado's 100-day enlistment was nearly up, and still it had done no fighting. In the saloons of Denver it was ridiculed as "The Bloodless Third." Chivington's political stock was falling. He apparently decided to use his regiment against any available Indians—and Black Kettle's village on Sand Creek was available.

Behind that cold-blooded decision was a man almost demented. "I long to be wading in gore!" Chivington had once exclaimed at a dinner party. To a would-be peacemaker who tried to engage him in rational argument, he announced that he was "on the warpath." And having determined to kill Indians, he made few distinctions among the Indians he meant to kill.

"Kill all you come across," he told his troops on one occasion. "I am fully satisfied," he said at another time, "that to kill them is the only way to have peace and quiet." One of the orders he snapped to his men before combat ran: "I want you to kill and scalp all, big and little!" He was fond of that odious rationalization used in the West as an excuse for murdering Indian children and babies: "Nits make lice!" Small wonder that a subordinate later described him as a "fiend incarnate."

With such a man at their head, the men of the combined 3rd and 1st knew full well what was expected of them. Moreover, they were not reluctant to implement their leader's most savage intentions. In the brief period since their enlistment, the troops had already shown themselves to be a rowdy lot who carried whiskey in their saddlebags, didn't bother to wear uniforms on campaign, and often refused to obey their officers.

These men rode into Fort Lyon through deep snow on November 28, and Chivington posted a guard with orders to kill anyone who tried to leave the post, lest the Indians be warned. Several officers at Fort Lyon who had been involved in the peace negotiations protested Chivington's plan to attack the village at Sand Creek, and he was enraged. The onetime preacher shook his big fist in a young officer's face and cried, "Damn any man who sympathizes with Indians! I have come to kill all Indians and I believe it is right to use any means under God's heaven!"

That night he rode out of Fort Lyon at 8 p.m. with more than 700 troops. The sky was clear, the stars bright, the air biting. Men went to their whiskey bottles for warmth. At dawn of the 29th they were within sight of Black Kettle's village, on a horseshoe bend of the creek. About 500 Indians were there, two thirds of them women and children. Most of the warriors were in hunting camps 50 miles away. Since the Indians believed themselves to be at peace, they had posted no guards other than boys tending the pony herd.

Chivington sent a company to seize the herd, so that no one could escape. The Indians, now aroused, watched in alarm. Black Kettle hastily raised his American flag on a tall lodgepole. Moments later, on the same pole, he raised a white flag of surrender. A part-Cheyenne scout who was with Chivington remembered the people huddling under the flags; he heard Black Kettle telling them that the soldiers would not hurt them while they were under the two flags. White Antelope, a chief of more than 70 years, hurried out to the soldiers. When he saw they were shooting, the scout heard him cry out in English, "Stop! Stop!" Then he stood with arms folded until the bullets brought him down.

The soldiers fired rifles, pistols, and cannon loaded with small shot. The people ran, scattering, shrieking and crying. The few warriors seized their weapons and gathered around the women and children, herding them up the creek bed. Black Kettle's wife was hit nine times; miraculously, she survived. As the soldiers charged through the camp, women pleading for mercy were shot down. Some 40 women in a cave sent out a girl about six years old with a white flag. She was shot and killed within a few steps. Then the soldiers dragged the women out and killed and scalped them.

One soldier fired at a child toddling in the sand and missed. "Let me try the son of a bitch," another said but he also missed. Grunting in disgust, a third soldier

In Robert Lindneux's *Sand Creek Massacre*, battle swirls around American and truce flags raised by the Indians in a gesture of peace.

took careful aim and killed the child. Babies' brains were dashed out against trees. An infant a few months old was tossed into a wagon's feedbox, left there all day and dropped on the prairie to die that night. The wounded were killed. Bodies were scalped and ripped open with knives. Someone cut off White Antelope's scrotum, planning to make a tobacco pouch of it. A woman's body was cut open; her unborn child was dropped on the ground beside her.

The Indians fled up the stream bed. When they came to a place with high banks, they tucked the women and children under the cover of the banks and turned to fight. The soldiers tried to dislodge them and failed. Finally, at nightfall the troops withdrew and these surviving Indians, Black Kettle among them, set out on foot in zero temperature, blood freezing on their wounds, for the hunting camps 50 miles away.

Ninety-eight Indian women and children and 25 men were killed that day. The soldiers lost nine killed and 38 wounded; some of their casualties were caused by the hail of careless fire that they themselves threw in all directions. Though Black Kettle and his wife survived this day, they died together four years later when George Armstrong Custer sneak-attacked the Indian chief's village on the Washita.

The 3rd Colorado—"The Bloody Third," now —rode back to Denver with more than 100 wet scalps, which were triumphantly displayed in a theater. The men were heroes for a while, but eventually the country came to realize the disgrace of the carnage at Sand Creek. A public clamor arose, a demand that the authorities unearth the truth, and three separate military and civilian commissions investigated the massacre. All condemned it, yet no one was brought to trial, mainly because no one remained in the military to be tried.

The 3rd was mustered out on December 28 and Chivington, too, soon left the service, putting everyone beyond reach of a court-martial. The only retribution was the destruction of Chivington's political career. With his reputation gone he drifted to California, then went back to Nebraska and finally to Colorado, there to spin out the rest of a long and inconsequential life. To the end of his days he repeated one astonishing, yet pathetic statement: "I stand by Sand Creek."

Such treachery as Chivington's convinced Indians everywhere that virtually no white man could be trusted.

They did, though, make a few exceptions; among them, oddly enough, was a general whom the ferocious Apaches regarded as their most dangerous antagonist. He was Lieutenant Colonel (and Brevet Major General) George Crook, assigned as commander of the Department of Arizona to pacify the Apaches. Yet Crook was known and admired by the Apaches as a man whose word could be trusted, and who even tended to fight in the traditional way of Indians, man to man and not by matching cannon against lances.

For Crook and his soldiers the Apache campaigns, fought in New Mexico and Arizona, were indeed very different from those on the Plains. Here the actions tended to be small-scale—murderous patrols amid arid mountains. Water was all but nonexistent, the trails so steep and narrow that horses and mules sometimes fell to their death and soldiers often chose to travel on foot.

There never were many Apaches—such country cannot support many people—but they were fierce fighters; Crook called them "the tiger of the human species." Major George Forsyth, hero of the Beecher's Island siege, described them as "cruel, crafty, wary, quick to scent danger, equally active to discover a weak or exposed place within reach, tireless when pursued, patient in defeat, and merciless in success." Apaches were in fact masters of trickery and treachery; but some white men like Crook, who knew them, admired them both as fighters and, occasionally, as trustworthy friends.

In the fall of 1872 settlers in Arizona suffered a series of lightning Apache raids. Typically the warriors darted down from mountain strongholds, killed and were gone. Crook was determined to strike at these remote bases, but no white men knew how to penetrate the distant reaches of the mountains. To get there soldiers would have to rely on a band of friendly Apaches whom Crook had enlisted as scouts.

The job of recruiting such scouts was not especially difficult. The Apaches were not a single cohesive tribe, but a loosely organized confederation of diverse bands and divisions. Some bands had long since cast their lot on the side of the white man; others came over temporarily as a result of intratribal warfare; in still others there were single warriors who for reasons of their own had decided to be friendly rather than hostile. General Crook, who called his scouts "the entering wedge in solution of this Apache question," never lacked for

Apaches to guide his troops in pursuit of their kin.

In late fall of 1872, some 220 of Crook's men from the 5th U.S. Cavalry set out under the command of Major William H. Brown. On December 27 they were camped at the base of the Superstition Mountains east of the village of Phoenix. Brown called his officers together and told them that one of their Apache scouts, a man named Nantaje, had once lived in a naturally fortified cave in the nearby Salt River Canyon. Nantaje believed the raiders were now using the place as both a base and a refuge, and he declared his willingness to lead the troops there.

The Salt River Canyon was some 1,200 feet deep; the usual passage through it ran along the riverbed at its bottom. Few men bothered to climb the mesa high above the river because nothing grew there, but from this mesa a secret trail led down the side of the chasm to the cave. The cave could, in fact, be reached only from above—which is why it had remained unknown to the soldiers, even though they long had suspected that Apaches had a hideout in the canyon.

Brown picked out all his able men, including Lieutenant John Bourke, an intelligent, articulate young officer who was later to write a vivid journal of the action upon which the following account is based. At 8 o'clock that night, according to Bourke, the soldiers left the camp wearing moccasins that had been stuffed with hay to ensure silence. They climbed the mesa on foot and at midnight reached the chasm's edge. In the chill of the desert night they wrapped their blankets about

Troops and Indian scouts attacking Skeleton Cave "pour in lead by the bucketful," in the words of an officer. Bullets aimed at the roof of the cave ricocheted off into the interior where besieged Apaches crouched.

them and waited, while the Indian scouts ranged ahead.

Nantaje had seen a flicker of light at the lip of the canyon and was sure the Apaches were near. In a depression where a spring fed a few spears of grass, he found some 15 trail-worn ponies and mules. The Apaches, he knew, had been raiding in the Gila Valley; he assumed that the ponies were part of the booty and that a raiding party had arrived just ahead of the soldiers. The Indians had gone into the canyon, leaving the horses behind them, but there was no way of knowing whether they had seen the soldiers first. If they had, it was certain that they would now be preparing an ambush. Prudently, Major Brown divided his forces, sending a column under the command of Captain James Burns to backtrack the raiders' trail. It would be Burns's

job to make sure that a second party of raiders did not come up on the rear of Brown's men, trapping them on the perilous trail above the Salt River.

The thin light of dawn was on the upper mesa when Brown's single file of about 100 men started down into the canyon. The trail was almost indistinguishable in some places, inches wide in others. Beside it yawned a thousand-foot abyss that the dawn had not yet penetrated. Each man watched the man before him, stepping slowly, carefully. Orders were passed along in whispers. The men paused at a level place, and some of the men said they doubted there were Indians here. Nantaje smiled. "Wait and see," he said. Brown told Lieutenant William J. Ross to take a dozen of the best shots and probe forward. In the lead, Nantaje and Ross picked their way silently down the trail until the scout suddenly stopped just before a sharp turn. He listened, then whispered, "Apaches."

Both men crawled to the turn and peeped around. The cave was only 40 yards away. It lay in a nook at another sharp turn in the trail, 500 feet below the level of the mesa, 700 feet above the riverbed. A small flat area at its mouth, little more than a widening of the trail, dropped off in a sheer cliff. At the cave mouth itself a natural parapet of smooth stone rose some 10 feet high, making the interior nearly impregnable.

The warriors returning from the raid had lighted fires and were singing and dancing as their women prepared food. The firelight flickered against the canyon's stone walls above; it was this tiny reflected flash of light that Nantaje had seen from the mesa above. Ross signaled his marksmen to follow around the corner. They eased themselves behind stones and each man chose the warrior that made his best target. On Ross's whispered command they fired in unison. Six warriors fell dead, and in the confusion of sudden noise and death the others dashed into the recesses of the cave.

The noise of the volley had reverberated through the chasm. On the trail above, Brown told Bourke to take the first 40 men in the line to Ross's relief at once. The men raced down the terrifying trail and turned the corner. In an instant they saw the whole picture—the shallow cave, the stone parapet, Ross and his men crouched behind rocks. They leaped to join them just as the Indians, recovering from their surprise, began firing. Bourke noted that the soldiers were 30 yards from the near side of the cave, 40 yards from the far side.

As Brown slowly brought the rest of his men down the trail, an Indian slipped away from the far side of the cave and climbed through the rocks, presumably headed for help. Far above, out of all normal rifle range, he paused and gave a triumphant yell. A 5th Cavalry blacksmith sighted on him and fired. It was an extraordinary shot, for it killed the distant warrior.

Brown now held his men in two groups, the first up forward with Ross and Bourke, the second guarding the rear. He checked their positions, satisfied himself that they could resist assault from the cave and told them to hold their fire. In the lull he called on the Apaches to surrender. From the cave came derisive shouts, which Nantaje translated for Brown: The soldiers were al-

ready dead men, this day was their last, tomorrow the crows and the buzzards would feast on their bodies.

These were not necessarily empty threats. The Apaches were equal to the soldiers in numbers, and the Indian position was such that the soldiers could not hope to assault it without scaling ladders; at that, an assault in force would have to climb 10 feet of smooth stone with weapons slung, only to face rifles, lances and arrows at the top. After dark, the Indians could slip out of their stronghold without penalty, move along the cliffs as readily as mountain goats and be in position to slaughter the soldiers at the dawn of the next day.

Oblivious to this uncomfortable possibility, Brown called again for the Indians to surrender. Again he was jeered. He asked them to let their women and children come out, and promised them kind treatment. This time, the Indians didn't even bother to answer him; instead they gave him a blast of bullets. The soldiers fired back, but with both sides well sheltered only one soldier was hit, while the Indians appeared as strong as ever. As the desert sun began to pour down into the canyon, it was obvious that the two forces were at an impasse.

Then someone noticed that the roof of the shallow cave sloped downward toward the back. Brown ordered the soldiers to fire at the roof of the cave just above the mouth. A hail of lead splattered deep into the cave, and Bourke could hear the cries of wounded, frightened Indians, including women and children. The Apaches rushed forward to crouch behind the natural stone parapet, but still the ricocheting, shattering slugs were hitting them. Momentarily Brown stopped the shooting and called again for them to surrender.

A wailing chant rose from the cave and Nantaje cried, "It is the death song; look out—here they come." About 20 warriors leaped up onto the rock parapet, firing rapidly. Half of them burst out of the far side of the parapet and made for the tumbled rocks. At this point the second line of soldiers, until now unnoticed by the Indians, opened fire, killing six or seven of the running men and driving the others back. Those on the parapet who were still alive tumbled back behind the rocks. Inside the death song continued.

Brown ordered his men to lay the heaviest possible fire against the cave roof and then prepare to charge. Under cover of fire, half the men would cross in front of the parapet to strike at the entrance from which the Indians had tried to escape. But just before this dangerous maneuver was attempted, the situation changed.

Back-trailing the Indians on the mesa above, Burns and his men had heard the heavy firing, for the noise carried easily in the dry desert air. They had turned back to the canyon and were soon on the chasm's edge directly above the cave. Peering down, they could see the Indians huddled behind the parapet and the string of soldiers along the face of the cliff. Up on the mesa, boulders bigger than cannonballs were everywhere. Burns's men rolled them to the edge of the chasm and tipped them over on signal. Suddenly, to the amazement of all below, a mass of stone thundered down into the cave. Some stones split when they struck, fragments flying like bullets. Boulders smashed bodies, then bounded over the parapet and on down to the river below. The noise drowned the death song and the sound of rifles. A thick dust hid the cave from the soldiers. When the stones stopped falling and the dust cleared, there was silence. The chanting had stopped.

Brown ordered a charge. It was like charging a cemetery, Bourke thought, yet no one could be sure that there wasn't a pocket in the cave in which survivors might be waiting. They dashed across the open ground, up the parapet, and into the entrance to face a horrible sight. Crushed bodies, some hardly recognizable as human, were everywhere. Scores were dead or dying, many of them women and children. Arms and legs protruded from rock piles. In all, 76 Apaches were killed that day; about 35 were still alive when the soldiers stormed the cave, but half of them were dying.

That afternoon the soldiers marched from Salt River Canyon with 18 captives, most of them wounded. The dead were simply left where they had fallen. Thirty-four years later, in 1906, a wandering cowboy found the skeletons and caused a minor sensation in Phoenix with his report. But even on that day in 1872 both the soldiers and the Indians knew they had passed through a pivotal episode in a war that had flickered meanly for over 20 years. Brown and his men had proved that soldiers could find and kill Apaches in their deepest retreats. Denied the cover of the mountains, the Indians gradually gave way under the grinding pressure of the campaign—and as long as Crook, with his hard-handed tactics and shrewd insights, remained in the field, the Apaches ceased to be a major threat in Arizona.

154

Apache scouts, like this fierce crew campaigning in the Southwest with the 6th Cavalry, often joined the Army straight from the warpath, hoping to use U.S. power to take revenge on their tribal enemies.

Scouts U.S. Army

5 | Future commanders of the West

As the Civil War drew to a close the five men shown here were headed for a time of drastic change. All five were posted to the West to fight Indians —but in the shrinking postwar Army only Sheridan kept his general's rank, overseeing nearly all major campaigns on the Plains through the mid-1880s.

As a colonel, James Forsyth led the 7th Cavalry at the Battle of Wounded Knee and eventually became a Major General. Wesley Merritt fought Indians for 10 years; he, too, regained his stars. But for the other two, the move West was a tragedy: Thomas Devin died from the rigors of campaigning; Custer perished in combat, idolized by the public but despised as a reckless fool by many of his fellow soldiers.

157

The strategy: "Kill or hang all warriors"

On a spring day in 1871, disquieting news came clacking over the telegraph wires and into the Chicago headquarters of the Army's Division of the Missouri. From the wire, Division commander Lieutenant General Philip Henry Sheridan, the second highest ranking officer in the American Army, learned that, 1,200 miles to the south, his only superior officer was traveling almost alone into Indian country. General William Tecumseh Sherman, the commanding general of the entire Army, the message read, had just left San Antonio, heading north along the Texas frontier to Fort Sill in the Indian Territory.

Sheridan knew that Sherman had been wanting to talk at first hand with Texas settlers who had been complaining to the Army of Indian depredations. Typically, the Commander in Chief did not convene a retinue of lesser generals and aides, nor demand a wagon train for his baggage. He detested the normal pomp of a general officer. Instead, he had commandeered an ambulance —the Army's equivalent of a stagecoach—called for a handful of soldiers for escort and struck north from San Antonio. He was traveling into Kiowa territory, as Phil Sheridan was well aware. From headquarters at Chicago, however, there was little that Sheridan could do but wish his commander the best of luck, hope the shaky peace with the Indians on the Texas border would last a little longer—and then wait to see how things turned out. Whatever happened, Sheridan would not know about it for days, perhaps weeks. For, once Sherman moved over the hill from the nearest telegraph wire, he was very much on his own on the Western

frontier, out of touch and possibly beyond rescue.

Meanwhile, apart from the adventurous impulses of his hard-nosed boss, Phil Sheridan had plenty of other worries. Throughout the 1870s he held the most important military command in the nation, the Division of the Missouri (map, page 163). This Division embraced a vast territory in which the United States Army did most of its Indian-fighting after the Civil War. The area included the jealously defended Sioux and Cheyenne hunting grounds on the northern Plains; the Rocky Mountains and the Black Hills, where these same tribes warred against encroaching goldminers; the southern Plains, where Kiowas and Comanches made slashing raids against settlers; and the stark mountain strongholds of the Apaches in New Mexico.

In this arena, hardly a week passed when someone, white or Indian, was not robbed, killed, kidnapped, burned out, cheated or otherwise encroached upon in the struggle for the Western land. The consequences and the responsibility for dealing with these depredations ultimately fell upon Phil Sheridan and his field officers in the Division of the Missouri. These men and their personalities, their reactions under the stresses of conflict, were a critical factor in the story of the war for the West. They affected—even controlled—its course. And in some of the battles, the top commanders were as involved and endangered as was any private soldier.

Sheridan's predecessor as Divisional commandant was none other than William Tecumseh Sherman, who had taken it over in 1866, two years after his infamous march through Georgia. Under Sherman, Sheridan had run the Division's hottest and most dangerous sector, the Department of the Missouri. In 1869, when Sherman stepped up to the command of the entire Army, Sheridan was in line for the higher post. In fact, his promotion was virtually assured, for Sheridan had a potent patron in Washington—the newly elected President,

Top Indian-fighter was cavalry hero Phil Sheridan, who in 1869 became commander of the Army's enormous Division of the Missouri. In this 1865 portrait he is framed by a tableau of his Civil War exploits.

This single page from the War Department's military registry of 1876 lists the entire U.S. Army of that year. Two thirds of the meager fighting force was off guarding forts and chasing Indians on the frontier.

30. Organization of the Army under the acts of June 16 and 23, 1874, March 2 and 3, 1875, and June 26, 1876.

	General officers.	Military secretary to Lieutenant-General.	Aides-de-camp to general officers.	Adjutant-General's Department.	Inspector-General's Department.	Bureau of Military Justice.	Quartermaster's Department.	Subsistence Department.	Medical Department.	Pay Department.	Corps of Engineers.	Ordnance Department.	Chief Signal Officer.	Post chaplains.	Ten regiments of cavalry.	Five regiments of artillery.	Twenty-five regiments of infantry.	Military Academy.	Noncommissioned staff, unattached to regiments.	Enlisted men unattached to regiments.	Indian scouts.	Total.	Signal detachment.	Retired officers.
COMMISSIONED OFFICERS.																								
General	1																					1		
Lieutenant-general	1																					1		
Major-generals	3																					3		7
Brigadier-generals	6			1		1	1	1	1	1	1	1										14		19
Colonels				2	b1		b4	2	6	2	6	3	1		10	5	25					67		52
Lieutenant-colonels		a1		4	2		8	3	10	2	12	4			10	5	25					a86		27
Majors				10	2	b4	14	8	50	50	24	10			30	15	25					242		36
Aides-de-camp		a29																				a29		
Captains							30	12	74		30	20			120	60	250					596		91
Adjutants (extra lieutenants)															10	5	25					40		
Regimental quartermasters (extra lieutenants)															10	5	25					40		
Battalion adjutant											c1											c1		
Battalion quartermaster											c1											c1		
First lieutenants									51		26	16			120	120	250					583		50
Second lieutenants									10						120	65	250					445		13
Additional second lieutenants																						(d)		
Chaplains														e30	e2		e2					e34		e3
Military storekeepers							(b)															(b)		
Ordnance storekeepers												(b)										(b)		
Medical storekeepers									(b)													(b)		
Total	11			17	5	5	57	26	192	55	109	54	1	30	432	280	877					2,151		
ENLISTED MEN.																								
Sergeant-majors															10	5	25					40		
Quartermaster-sergeants															10	5	25					40		
Chief musicians															10	5	25					40		
Principal musicians																10	50					60		
Saddler sergeants															10							10		
Chief trumpeters															10							10		
Ordnance sergeants																			115			115		
Commissary-sergeants																			f148			148		
Hospital stewards									79													79		
Battalion sergeant-major											1											1		
Battalion quartermaster-sergeant											1											1		
First sergeants															120	60	250					430		
Sergeants											20	40			600	250	1,000					1,910	150	
Corporals											16	80			480	240	1,000					1,816	30	
Trumpeters															240							240		
Musicians											8					120	500					628		
Farriers and blacksmiths															240							240		
Artificers																120	500					620		
Saddlers															120							120		
Master wagoners																						(g)		
Wagoners															120	60	250					g430		
Privates (first class)											80	150										230		
Privates (second class)											74	130										204		
Privates															6,480	1,725	8,460					16,665	220	
Total									79		200	400			8,450	2,600	12,085		263	623	300	25,000	400	
Military Academy:																								
Professors																		9				9		2
Cadets																		312				312		
Aggregate	11			17	5	5	57	26	271	55	309	454	1	30	8,882	2,880	12,962	321	263	623	300	27,472	400	300

a The military secretary and the 29 aides-de-camp, belonging also to corps or regiments in the strength of which they are included, are excluded as staff officers from the "total commissioned" and "aggregate."

b The several acts of Congress reorganizing the staff corps provides that no officer shall be reduced in rank or mustered out of service by reason of any provisions of said acts. The number allowed by law is given in the above table, and there is in service in excess of the authorized number as follows: 4 colonels, inspectors-general; 8 majors, judge-advocates; 1 colonel, assistant quartermaster-general; 7 captains, military storekeepers in quartermaster's department; 4 captains, medical storekeepers, and 11 ordnance storekeepers.

c The adjutant and quartermaster of the battalion of engineers, being included in the strength of their corps, are excluded as staff officers from the "total commissioned" and "aggregate."

d One additional second lieutenant is allowed to each company in the service.

e The chaplains to the colored regiments and the post chaplains rank as captain of infantry.

f One commissary-sergeant for each military post or place of deposit of subsistence supplies.

g Master wagoners and wagoners limited to the exigencies of the service.

One veterinary surgeon at $75 per month is allowed to each regiment of cavalry, and to each of the Ninth and Tenth regiments an additional veterinary surgeon at $100 per month. Being viewed as civilians, they are excluded from the table.

A superintendent to each national cemetery. Being viewed as civilians, they are not included in the table.

Indian scouts to the number of 1,000 may be employed with pay, etc., of cavalry soldiers.

The act of June 16, 1874, limits the number of enlisted men to 25,000, including Indian scouts and excepting the signal service.

Ulysses Grant. Grant had never forgotten Sheridan's effectiveness in the Civil War, when Sheridan's cavalry had turned Lee's flank and boxed in the great Southern general until he had no choice but to surrender at Appomattox. Partly in gratitude, Grant handed the Division of the Missouri to Sheridan. He was never sorry; years later, reviewing Sheridan's performance, Grant said: "I believe General Sheridan has no superior as a general either living or dead, and perhaps not an equal."

Sheridan surely did not look the part. He was a small man with abnormally long arms; and, his official portraitists notwithstanding *(pages 156, 158)*, his daily uniform was any old, mismatched, rumpled set of clothes. Preferring their generals in the heroic mold, people tended to be disappointed by Sheridan's appearance. A little fellow like you, an old farmer once marveled, how could you run an Army? Sheridan just smiled. Moreover, he had a massive, oddly shaped head; one biographer reports that the larger part lay forward of his ears, so it was difficult for him to keep his hat on. Thus his most violent charges were made bareheaded, because his hat fell off — though his admirers preferred to attribute these bareheaded charges to gallantry.

Lawyer George Templeton Strong of New York City, who once invited Sheridan to dinner, later described him as "a stumpy, quadrangular little man, with a forehead of no promise and hair so short that it looks like a coat of black paint. But his eyes and mouth show force." He feared that Sheridan would be a boring guest, but found him instead a lively conversationalist. And when dinner was over Sheridan swept one of the prettiest young women present off to the theater.

Strong should not have been surprised, for along with command, Sheridan relished the good life. By the time he took over the Division of the Missouri and moved its headquarters from St. Louis to the more cosmopolitan city of Chicago, he was established as an accomplished, if minor, bon vivant. He enjoyed the theater; he was a regular guest at dinners that steadily reshaped his figure, so that he got rounder and rounder; and he loved to go to dances. Once he is said to have lured Grant himself onto the dance floor; as the music quickened, Sheridan whirled his partner away and left his clumsy President to stumble to the sidelines.

But this frank enjoyment of the fruits of success was only part of the man. In the field there was nothing soft

or playful about Phil Sheridan. A restless, irritable soldier, he forgave few mistakes, including his own. On the way to command of the Division he had marched with his troops, eaten with them, and rarely allowed himself the comforts of the warm tents and personal service that his own junior officers often insisted on for themselves. During a bitter march in 1868, when a blizzard blew down the tents of a Kansas volunteer regiment, the men found their general shivering under a wagon for the night. A member of that regiment later described Sheridan as "marching at our head in snow and rain, enduring all the hardships of wind and weather." The same youth also observed approvingly that Sheridan was "quite jovial, and does not put on much style."

He was very much at ease in the company of the frontiersmen he met on the campaign trail, and had a particular admiration for his scouts, who played a critical role both in sniffing out the enemy and in acting as message carriers. Sheridan's personal favorite was the redoubtable William F. (Buffalo Bill) Cody who, during that frigid campaign in 1868, made a heroic series of horseback rides totaling some 350 miles in about 60 hours. Cody's epic feat began with a 65-mile ride from Fort Larned to Fort Hays — in his memoirs Sheridan recalled that the route was "infested with Indians." From Hays, Buffalo Bill set off for Fort Dodge, 95 miles away (Sheridan noted that "several couriers had been killed" on that stretch). From Dodge, Bill rode back to his own post at Larned, and from Larned he galloped out to meet Sheridan again at Hays. The dispatches he carried told Sheridan exactly what he needed to know — the location of the Cheyenne winter camps in 1868 — and proved a key to a successful campaign.

Sheridan was also notorious in his low tolerance for fools, which he was likely to express in barrack-room phrases. On one Western campaign he called for Buffalo Bill to go on a reconnaissance, unaware that Cody had been sent off with dispatches. Another scout, suffering from a severe case of hero worship for Cody, presented himself to Sheridan, crying, "I'm Buffalo Bill when he's away!" Sheridan glared at him. "The hell you are," he growled, and promptly gave him a nickname; euphemized to Buffalo Chips, it stuck to that scout for the rest of his life.

Ultimately, with good scouts or bad, accountability for whatever happened fell upon Phil Sheridan. It was he, along with Sherman, who made the major decisions and conceived the strategy that ultimately destroyed the Plains Indians. It was a cruel strategy, the so-called winter campaign *(pages 36-38)*, aimed at women and children, as well as at warriors. And Sheridan could be barbarous in seeing that it was carried out. His orders to George Custer, when he sent him out against Black Kettle's village on the Washita, speak for themselves: "Kill or hang all warriors and bring back all women and children." Such orders could only lead to one end: the utter destruction of the Indian enemy.

But Sheridan's plans were repeatedly frustrated. They were frustrated by lack of communications, poor intelligence, simple human failure — or by the downright orneriness of his own superior officer, William Tecumseh Sherman. In fact Sherman's foray, begun that spring morning in 1871, was a superb example of just how wrong things could go in the confused, far-flung struggle between the soldiers and the Indians.

Sherman's ambulance rolled northeast across Texas until it approached Fort Richardson in the vicinity of the Trinity River. Near the river the little party rode unknowingly and unscathed through a carefully laid ambush of more than a hundred Kiowa warriors. Much later, the reason for their escape became known. The Kiowas had consulted a spiritual leader who, after seeking and obtaining a vision of the future, had given instructions for their ambush. There would be two parties on the road, he said. The first would be small and weak in appearance. It would be a tempting target, but they must not attack it; they must wait for the second.

The first party, as it turned out, was Sherman's small detachment. The second was a wagon supply train, laden with corn and fodder and driven by a dozen teamsters. The Kiowas swooped down, killed seven of the men and rode off with the cargo. That night the five survivors crept into Fort Richardson to report.

Sherman was enraged by this violation of the peace. The Indians saw the attack quite differently, as a justifiable retaliation for many wrongs. Their land had been taken, their treaty agreements had not been honored, their Government rations had been stolen, their pride was assaulted — naturally, they struck back. They certainly did not view the attack as some sort of crime. But that is exactly how Sherman saw it, basing his reaction on a directive that he and Sheridan had extracted from Washington. The new rule said that, despite the solemn treaties of the past, Indians would henceforth be dealt with as individuals. Thus, in a case of this sort, they would be treated as criminals rather than members of an enemy army or subjects of nations with which the United States would negotiate.

This tough-minded, uncomplicated policy was typical of Sherman, whose entire life — and success — had been built upon the uncompromising use of force. Dur-

THE VAST BATTLEGROUND OF THE PLAINS

One of the biggest U.S. war theaters ever commanded by a single American general was Phil Sheridan's Military Division of the Missouri, which embraced four sprawling Departments, each bigger than New England and each with its own subordinate headquarters. Sheridan described the Division in 1874 as covering "more than one million square miles of frontier country," and containing "within its limits ninety-nine Indian tribes, numbering about 192,000 persons." Its Army personnel consisted of "seventy-six established posts and camps, garrisoned by eight regiments of cavalry, seventeen regiments of infantry, and a small detachment of engineer troops, aggregating, at the last official report, 17,819 commissioned officers and enlisted men."

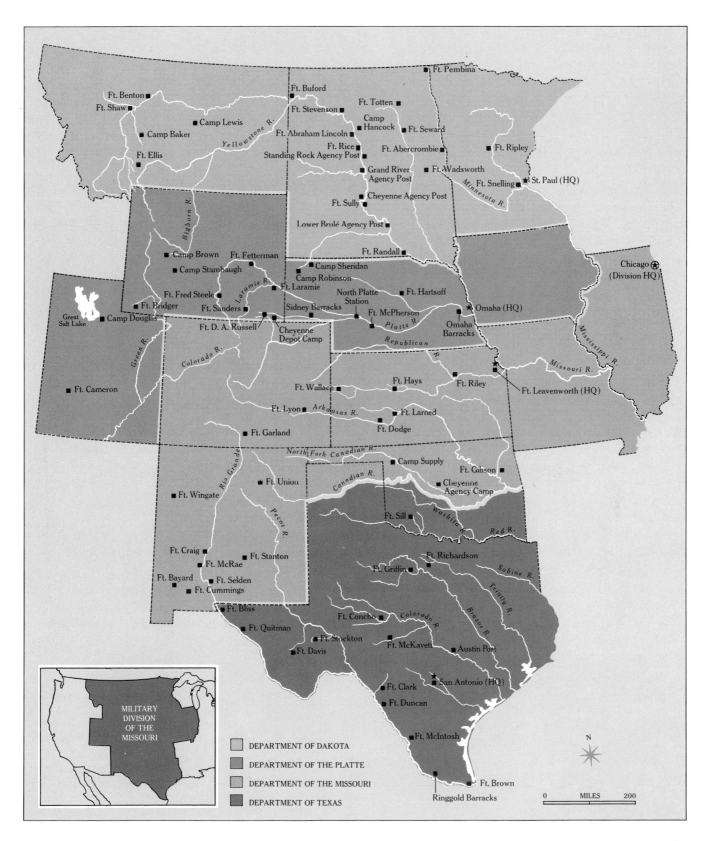

Ft. Pembina

Ft. Benton
Ft. Shaw
Camp Lewis
Camp Baker
Ft. Ellis

Ft. Buford
Ft. Stevenson
Ft. Totten
Camp Hancock
Ft. Seward

Ft. Abraham Lincoln
Ft. Rice
Standing Rock Agency Post
Ft. Abercrombie
Ft. Ripley

Yellowstone R.

Grand River Agency Post
Ft. Wadsworth
Ft. Snelling
St. Paul (HQ)

Cheyenne Agency Post
Ft. Sully

Bighorn R.

Lower Brulé Agency Post

Minnesota R.

Chicago
(Division HQ)

Camp Brown
Camp Stambaugh
Ft. Fetterman
Camp Sheridan
Camp Robinson

Ft. Randall

Ft. Fred Steele
Ft. Laramie
Ft. Hartsuff

Ft. Bridger
Ft. Sanders
North Platte Station
Sidney Barracks
Omaha (HQ)

Great Salt Lake
Camp Douglas
Ft. D. A. Russell
Cheyenne Depot Camp
Ft. McPherson
Omaha Barracks

Laramie R.

Platte R.

Green R.

Colorado R.

Republican R.

Missouri R.

Ft. Leavenworth (HQ)

Mississippi R.

Ft. Cameron

Ft. Wallace
Ft. Hays
Ft. Riley

Ft. Lyon
Arkansas R.
Ft. Larned

Ft. Garland
Ft. Dodge

North Fork Canadian R.

Rio Grande

Camp Supply
Ft. Gibson

Ft. Union
Cheyenne Agency Camp

Ft. Wingate

Canadian R.

Pecos R.

Ft. Sill
Washita R.

Red R.

Ft. Craig
Ft. Stanton
Ft. Richardson
Sabine R.

Ft. McRae
Ft. Griffin

Ft. Bayard
Ft. Selden
Ft. Cummings

Trinity R.

Ft. Bliss
Ft. Concho
Colorado R.
Brazos R.

Ft. Quitman
Ft. Stockton
Ft. McKavett
Austin Post

Ft. Davis

San Antonio (HQ)

Ft. Clark
Ft. Duncan

N

Ft. McIntosh

Ft. Brown

Ringgold Barracks

MILITARY
DIVISION
OF THE
MISSOURI

DEPARTMENT OF DAKOTA

DEPARTMENT OF THE PLATTE

DEPARTMENT OF THE MISSOURI

DEPARTMENT OF TEXAS

0   MILES   200

In this 1878 photomontage made up of individual pictures cut out and pasted against a painted background, General Philip Sheridan takes a

regal seat in front of his Division of the Missouri staff officers as his horse, Winchester, stands unflinching a few feet from a booming cannon.

This regimental flag was carried through the Indian wars by all U.S. troops. While the cavalry version measured a modest five square feet, the flagmen of the infantry staggered under a 40-square-foot behemoth.

ing the Civil War he had proved himself an excellent organizer and a fine tactician. But it was his natural hardness and his faith in force that led to the savage march through Georgia. He had no patience with diplomacy or the subtleties of negotiation. Moreover he despised big cities, especially Washington, with its politicians and other institutions that seemed to him designed chiefly to give him trouble.

Five years after becoming Commanding General of the Army, Sherman had moved his headquarters—and with it, the headquarters of the command structure—to St. Louis. The grateful people of that city had presented him with a home there after the Civil War; and, what was more important, St. Louis was still a gateway to the West. To his brother John he wrote, "I

don't care so much about St. Louis—any place out West is more to my family than Washington"; and after a couple of hot St. Louis summers he confessed to John that he was "half disposed to move further West."

To his comrades in arms Sherman's move to St. Louis was an irresponsible jump that left the Army with no command presence in Washington. Angrily, Phil Sheridan wrote his commander: "Are you, as head of the Army, at liberty to break us down because you have been or may be subjected to annoyance in Washington?" (Eventually Sheridan succeeded Sherman as Commander of the Army; so at this point he may have been protecting ground he expected to occupy.)

Sherman stayed where he was—at least for a while. Besides loathing Washington and its slick politicians,

166

he had carried on a lifelong romance with the American West. He had gone to California as a young West Pointer during the Mexican War, and though he saw no fighting, he saw plenty of country. He liked it, was comfortable with its free and open people and its direct ways. Sometimes, around a prairie campfire he even fell into a mood of laughter and storytelling. He conceived an overpowering faith in the West, which he saw as both the future and the salvation of the United States.

There was only one thing wrong with the West, one impediment to settlement: the Indians. Never mind that the Indians were there first. And never mind that given a reasonable audience they might have negotiated some of the disputes. When chiefs assembled at one conference in Fort Laramie and told Sherman that they wanted peace but their impetuous young men were sometimes unmanageable, he was angered. Nodding at the chiefs he snapped, "Tell the rascals so are *mine;* and if another white man is scalped in all this region, it will be *impossible* to hold *mine* in."

Sherman did not truly want to hold his in, for basically he considered Indians as "a class of savages" who would soon be "displaced by the irresistible progress of our race." If the Indians resisted, he had confidence in his young men, with their superior equipment, to exterminate the rascals. His singlemindedness in this was a little appalling. For example, although Sherman recognized the railroad as an instrument of peaceful prosperity, he also saw it as being a splendid auxiliary killing machine. The ability of the roads to haul masses of troops day and night at speeds over 25 miles an hour led Sherman to exclaim, "I regard this railroad as the solution of 'our Indian affairs.'"

Against this background, Sherman's reaction to the Kiowa raid that so narrowly missed him in northern Texas was blunt and predictable. When Sherman reached Fort Sill on his long southern swing, he invited Satanta, the Kiowa chief who had led the raid, to a parley. Satanta attended. On the broad veranda of the headquarters building at Fort Sill, Satanta readily admitted the raid and in fact began to boast of it. Suddenly, Sherman broke in, telling him that he was under arrest and would be tried for murder. "I'd rather be dead," Satanta growled, and reached for the gun he carried under his blanket. The building's shutters flew open to reveal soldiers with their rifles trained on the chief.

He was taken back to Texas in irons, tried there for murder and found guilty.

The state was preparing to execute Satanta when horrified civilian proponents of a policy of appeasing the Indians prevailed on the Texas governor, who commuted the sentence to life imprisonment. Satanta was a leading Kiowa chief, and his execution by whites might have set off a series of vengeance killings. Sherman was furious; and the Indians were scarcely mollified. They considered imprisonment to be a hopelessly barbaric practice. And so the anger, fear and urge for revenge that was in the tribes grew more intense, making Sheridan's situation hotter than ever. They were not allayed when Satanta was released in 1873, for that act sent Sherman into yet another rage. He dashed off a letter to the governor of Texas predicting an Indian rampage in which the governor's scalp would be the first taken. Sherman never did get the hang of political discourse.

Nor could he quite absorb the vast and frustrating differences between fighting conventional Civil War battles, complete with intelligence and convenient supplies, and chasing a shrewd, mobile band of Indians across the largely trackless frontier. And this failure, too, caused Phil Sheridan and his troops many a grim month.

Again and again, in attempting to implement the punishing strategy Sherman so admired, Phil Sheridan would aim men in the supposed direction of Indians, hoping the troops would be able to find a trail and follow it to a village. But again and again a column would blunder about half lost for days on end, and finally return without ever having seen the enemy. Sometimes it was more than a column, and more than half lost.

One November an entire regiment, the 19th Kansas Cavalry, set out from Camp Beecher to meet Sheridan at Fort Supply, about 150 miles away, with five days' rations. After a week, their supplies exhausted, the weary regiment was utterly lost and in the midst of a howling blizzard. They stumbled through canyons and over snow-covered plains, while the little general worried and fumed, completely uncertain of their whereabouts. Then the regiment split up — a risky move at the best of times — with the strongest men going ahead. Five hundred men of the advance troops finally reached Fort Supply on November 28; the others, 600 starving men, did not straggle in till December. The regiment lost 700 of its horses to starvation and exposure. ◉

A cartoonist's crusade in defense of the Army

In his most savage mood, Nast depicted Indian raiders adorned with wholly fictitious wolf masks attacking an Army supply column.

In the 1870s, the Army fought campaigns on two fronts—against Indians in the West, and a penny-pinching Congress in Washington. To the delight of military men, the great political cartoonist Thomas Nast came to their aid on the Potomac front with a series of bitter drawings aimed straight at the nation's legislators.

The son of a Bavarian army musician who emigrated to America, Nast was loyal to the military all his life. His first major assignment—at age 19—was to depict Garibaldi's invasions of Sicily and Naples for the *New York Illustrated News.* Returning home on the eve of the Civil War, the young artist sketched such battle scenes as the bloody Union triumph at Gettysburg. His staunchly patriotic drawings, published in *Harper's Weekly,* were so stirring that President Lincoln called Nast "our best recruiting sergeant."

A decade later, when Nast again picked up his pen in defense of the colors, the U.S. Army had been cut to some 25,000 poorly equipped and underpaid men; Democratic congressmen were calling for a further reduction to 20,000 or even 15,000. A master at inventing political symbols (in one cartoon he created the Republican elephant), Nast represented the Army as a skeleton in uniform. With his sardonic drawings of Indians exploiting the Army's weakness, he tried to rally public opinion behind the military. In gratitude 3,500 soldiers and sailors dug up a quarter each from their own meager savings for a testimonial—an inscribed silver vase in the shape of a canteen.

Informed by a tearful Columbia (a frequent symbol for the American people) of a new and miserly military appropriations bill, the skeleton Army prepares to commit suicide.

Entangled in red tape, the skeleton Army still manages to protect frontier stations and refugee settlers against menacing Indians.

This vitriolic Nast cartoon protesting parsimonious military appropriations links the Democratic Party with a resurgent Confederacy.

Though officers' quarters at some Western stations were only sod huts, on a few posts the ranking men had comforts surpassing those of home. These are the furnishings of a colonel's parlor at Arizona's Fort Bowie.

The colonels and lieutenant colonels who led regiments in the field presented Sheridan with other problems. While he struggled with his own workload, his foiled strategies — and his impulsive commander — subordinates made many of the pivotal decisions that led to victories and defeats. And the simple fact was that on the Plains most of these men were not up to their jobs. They had come to professional maturity during the Civil War. Since then their stars, quite literally, had fallen. (In the postwar Army an astounding number of captains, majors and colonels were entitled to be addressed as general because of brevet or temporary rank they had held in the heat of that war.) They had played the first half of their lives on a great stage, only to spend the next 30 years in an often inglorious struggle against what many of them regarded as a bunch of filthy savages.

These men, who had known high position but were now reduced to field grade, jousted for the few promotions available. Feuds developed over who should

have this command or that. Many of these feuds dated back to the Civil War, but they still flourished. In 1869 Phil Sheridan himself happened to murmur a greeting to General William Averell, whom he had relieved of command at the Civil War battle of Fisher's Hill five years earlier. Next morning he got a stiff note from Averell, reading in part, "I cannot permit you to entertain the impression I am willing to resume friendly intercourse with you."

Sheridan's enemies claimed that Generals George H. Thomas and George G. Meade had died of broken hearts when Sheridan was handed the command of the Division of the Missouri. The charge was absurd (Thomas had actually died of a stroke in the act of writing a furious attack upon still another Civil War general, John M. Schofield; Meade died of pneumonia). But Sheridan inherited admirers of both these men in his Division, and had to manage with them. At times it seemed half his officers were not speaking to the other half; and assigning men to duty posts became as com-

plicated as arranging dinner parties in Washington without fanning the feuds, current and past.

In this competitive, angry situation, about the only chance for an ambitious man to make a real reputation — and with it, perhaps, those precious stars — was in combat. And the only combat was with Indians on the frontier. So despite the harsh living conditions, many officers sought frontier duty, and when they arrived they yearned for a chance to strike Indians. Most of them got their chance, and seized it with a vigor that should have delighted their Division commander in Chicago. Yet somehow they usually did not work out: the field officers reporting to Sheridan remained a surprisingly undistinguished lot. A typical and tragic situation was the one at Fort Phil Kearny in 1866, where the two officers in command spent most of their time sniping at one another. When battle was joined, one of them, Captain Fetterman, proved a fool; the other, Colonel Carrington, was weak (*pages 135-143*). That situation was extreme only in the scope of the disaster in which

it ended. Almost everywhere the officers' capacity for jealousy outstripped their military abilities.

One of the exceptions to this generally bleak command picture was George Crook, who made his mark in campaigns against the Apaches. Crook knew the importance of a combat reputation, and he kept his own well burnished. Newspaper correspondents accompanied his every move, and in addition he was blessed by two of the ablest Army memoirists of the period, Captains John Bourke and Charles King. Bourke, for instance, described him as "a beacon of hope to the settler and a terror to the tribes in hostility" — but both left accurate records of his campaigns.

Bourke and King had good material to work with. Eventually William T. Sherman himself was to call George Crook "the greatest Indian fighter and manager the army of the United States ever had." At the same time, Crook was the most decent and humane of the top officers in the West, a thoughtful, imaginative man who saw his enemies as humans rather than savages to

An officer at Fort Bowie, Arizona, snoozes on a veranda built by enlisted men. One officer who disliked the practice of using soldiers as laborers wrote feelingly of "the poor wretch who enlisted to quell hostile Indians" and wound up "doing odd jobs of plastering."

174

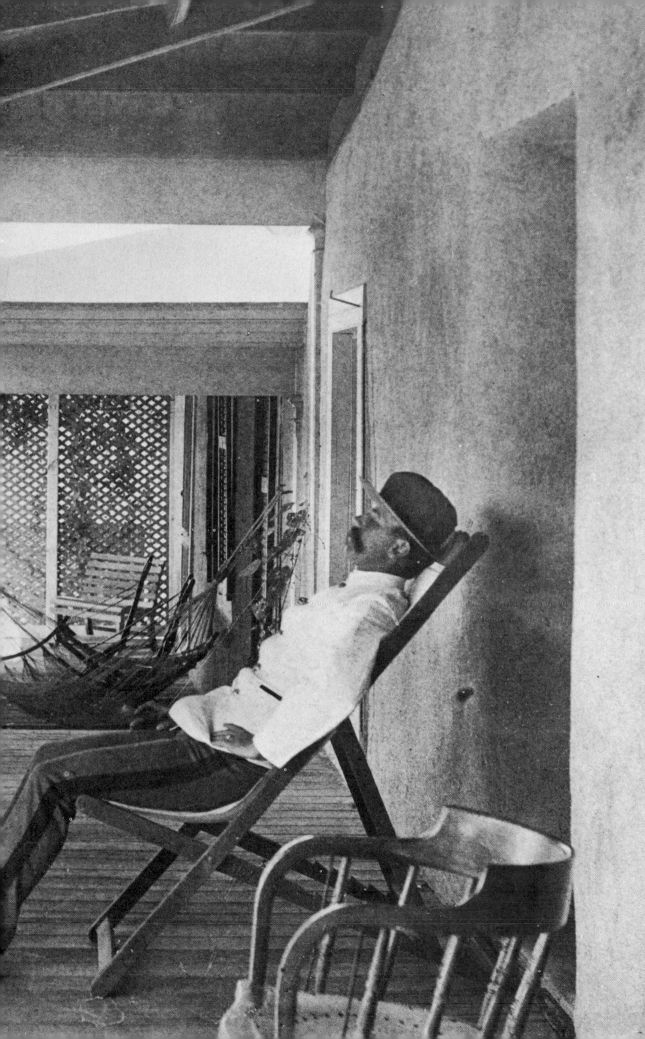

be destroyed. Moreover, Crook understood in many ways the Indians' predicament. "The American Indian," he once remarked, "commands respect for his rights only as long as he inspires terror for his rifle." And he dealt honorably with his foe, which is more than could be said for Sherman or Sheridan.

Crook was also a confirmed eccentric. He rode to war on a favorite mule *(page 178)*, sporting a magnificent forked beard and affecting a cork helmet and a white canvas suit of the sort usually worn by cavalrymen on stable detail. He was an avid hunter and would range far ahead of his column in search of game, even in dangerous country. Photographers found it easy to get him to pose in Napoleonic style, with one hand slipped into his blouse—and if his foot could be poised on the head of a newly downed antelope or grizzly, so much the better.

Some of Crook's eccentricities had their basis in hard common sense. For example, he lavished unprecedented care and love upon the humble army mule—because he understood the logistics of frontier warfare. With special harnesses and meticulous loading procedures, he induced his pack mules to carry up to 320 pounds apiece —about twice the usual army mule load and comparable to the 500 pounds that became the standard load of the elephants used by the British army in India. The great range of movement Crook gained by the use of these animals was one of the keys to his success.

Soldiers enjoyed serving under Crook. They liked him and tolerated his puritanical streak: Crook did not smoke; did not drink even coffee, let alone spirits; and was never heard to swear. And they contemplated the quirks of his character (including his love of publicity) with positive enjoyment. An affectionate ballad included a verse on the pleasures of a Crook mulepacker:

> I'd like to be a packer,
> And pack with George F. Crook,
> And dressed up in my canvas suit,
> To be for him mistook.
> I'd braid my beard in two forked tails,
> And idle all the day
> In whittling sticks and wondering
> What the New York papers say.

But the same soldiers, in another more sardonic ballad, reminded the general that Indian-fighting involved a good deal more than just mulepackers and mule trains:

> But you know full well that in your fights
> No soldier lad was slow,
> And it wasn't the packer that won ye a star
> In the Regular Army O.

Crook gained that star by a spectacular promotion from lieutenant colonel to brigadier general, at a time when virtually no one else was moving upward at all. In 1871, while Sherman was arresting Satanta at Fort Sill, President Grant named Crook commander of the Department of Arizona despite his comparatively low rank. Grant acted after a series of military disasters in the Southwest had left the Army in disarray and the settlers terrified. Within months Crook organized a detachment of friendly Apache scouts to lead the troops into the desert and mountain country. Soon afterward he ordered a series of columns to probe for hostiles.

One of the resulting encounters was the wild battle in Salt River Canyon *(pages 150-154)*. After the Salt River a sizable Apache camp in the Superstition Mountains surrendered to Crook and came onto a reservation. And in the following year, 1873, Crook won a victory over the last big concentration of free Apache warriors, on a plateau called Turret Butte. In one night Crook's troops clambered up the sides of this natural fortification. At dawn, with the Apaches surrounded, trumpets sounded the attack and rifles rang out. Some warriors were killed immediately; others killed themselves by leaping onto the rocks below; the remainder gave themselves up to their fork-bearded enemy.

Crook had earned his star. Now, as a general, he turned to a brief period of peacemaking, and helped the Apaches as no Indian agent nor surely any other general had ever dreamed of doing. He persuaded some of the fierce nomads to become shepherds and farmers, and found them good land on which to follow their new occupations. On this semiarid country, he encouraged the Indians to divert streams and dig irrigation ditches; he even helped set up a system to market the Indians' wool and meat and produce. So far as he was able, Crook worked for a lasting peace in the Southwest.

But he had won his reputation as an Indian-fighter, and an Indian-fighter he remained. It was Crook's Arizona campaign that led Sherman to rate him his best field commander. Phil Sheridan, too, noted Crook's suc-

Eccentric but effective, General George Crook wore an ostrich-feathered dress chapeau for this portrait. But in the field *(overleaf)* he was a down-to-earth officer who had his men's respect and got the job done.

Dressed for comfort on the trail and accompanied by two Apache scouts, General Crook sets off into the desert wearing a sun helmet and a light canvas jacket, and riding one of the mules he preferred to horses.

cess, and determined to use him in the Division of the Missouri. To some extent, Sheridan's decision ran against his own inclinations: he disliked Crook personally, and considered him soft on Indians. In return, Crook regarded Sheridan as unnecessarily cruel and vindictive, and disliked the very sight of the man himself. Years later, he spoke of the "bloated little carcass" of his well-fed commanding general.

Crook also hated and was reciprocally hated by another officer of great potential. This was Nelson Miles, one of the few non-West Pointers to excel on the western Plains, and a man whose energy was equaled only by his ambition. Miles had been a 22-year-old dry-goods clerk when the Civil War began (as West Pointers all through the Army reminded each other with sniffs); and what was worse to the regulars, he had purchased a commission. Nevertheless he had risen to the rank of brevet major general on obvious merit, and after the war was given a regular Army colonelcy and the command of the 5th Infantry in Kansas. He married

Sherman's niece, and his critics saw his marriage as self-promoting. In truth, it was a genuine love match and may actually have slowed Miles's career, because Sherman was anxious to avoid the charge of favoritism. But Sherman's attitude did not matter, anyway; Miles was determined to succeed and he stridently demanded every opportunity to prove himself.

In fact when Crook won his brigadier's star, Miles was livid with jealousy. He wrote Sherman that the promotion should have gone to him. The fact that the frontier was full of West Pointers who believed the same of themselves did not slow Miles's furious complaints. There he was, stuck in command of the 5th; the years were slipping by without providing him with any real chances to seize fame or rank.

Actually Nelson Miles was a field officer to Phil Sheridan's particular taste. He drove men hard, but he liked to talk shop with them and drank with them in off-duty hours. He attacked Indian encampments (when he could find them) with unbridled ferocity and gave little concern to the humanity of his enemies. And he got his chance at last in 1874, when Sheridan moved to break the power of the tribes on the southern Plains.

By 1874 a Washington-bred policy of relatively easy treatment for the Indians was collapsing in a mess of corruption and growing Indian unrest. After Satanta's release from a Texas penitentiary in 1873 — the move that so enraged Sherman — Indian raids became increasingly frequent and violent. Frontier settlements were in an uproar and the situation was coming to the point of explosion. In response, Phil Sheridan prepared for what he hoped could be a big and final fight. In August 1874 he launched four separate columns of troops against the Indians living in Texas and the tribal lands directly to the north.

Heading one of the columns, Nelson Miles finally found himself on a path that could lead to high command. From the start he drove his men to the limit. One example was the incident at the Red River in August of 1874 when Miles's men, plagued by thirst, literally cut their arms with knives to wet their swollen, breaking lips with their own blood *(pages 109, 114)*. Yet despite these ferocious demands Miles fought his battles by the book. He abandoned the pursuit at the Red River for sound military reasons: his lines of communication and supply were growing dangerously thin. By such prudence he managed to win himself a reputation both as a careful operator as well as an effective fighter. And as the campaign went on, Miles's men stayed in the forefront of it.

A manifestation of Miles's own calm, well-focused personality during those hard days is preserved in a stream of letters that Miles sent to his wife, Mary. Night after night, having seen to his men and to the planning of the next day's march, he would sit down at the ammunition box he used as a desk and write to his Mary. His letters are filled with a never-ending zeal to get the command "working the way I want it."

"I have to be Captain and Sergeant and Wagon Master and a little of everything," he wrote, "but I think I will get matters straightened out." Like Phil Sheridan himself, he had trouble with his staff: "I find altogether too many incompetent and inefficient officers who have no interest in their duties." But more and more often he was able to report success in what really counted: "We chased the Indians a very long distance, routed them

RESOLUTIONS.

JOINT RESOLUTION

Of thanks to General George Crook.

Be it resolved by the Legislative Assembly of the Territory of Arizona:

That the thanks of the people of Arizona Territory are due, and through their Representatives in the Eighth Legislative Assembly, are hereby tendered to that gallant soldier, Brigadier-General George Crook and the officers and men under his command, for the noble services they have rendered the country in subduing the hordes of hostile Indians that had, until the advent of General Crook in our Territory, held the country under a reign of terror, and civilization in check.

That we recognize the fact that the policy that General Crook has pursued has been the means, and the only means, that could have effected the final grand achievements of peace within our Territory, and immunity from depredations from the savages. Making war as he has with vigor, when war had to be waged, and being merciful and just at all times to those in his power, he has not only commanded the respect but won the esteem of the savages themselves.

That the Secretary of the Territory be instructed to transmit a copy of these resolutions to General Crook and the Secretary of War, and to all the papers printed in this Territory.

APPROVED February 12th, 1875.

out of their camps, whipped them in a good running fight, and scattered them in every direction."

In time Miles indeed got his units working the way he wanted, and inflicted a disaster upon the tribes. He maneuvered them into battles; he destroyed their villages, killed their horses, burned their food and clothing. Finally, they surrendered in droves. And then Sheridan dictated the fate of the captives. He convened a five-man commission at Fort Sill, gravely took evidence, found 75 leaders and subleaders guilty and deported them from their high, dry Plains to the distant swamps around St. Augustine, Florida.

With this harsh stroke major Indian resistance on the southern Plains ended for good — although with George Crook reassigned to the Department of the Platte, the mountain Apaches would rise again for 11 more years of sporadic fighting. Meanwhile tough little Phil Sheridan was preparing to try a similar series of strokes against the Indians on the northern Plains. But there the fighting was to prove vastly more difficult than it

Straight-eyed and tough, Colonel Nelson A. Miles communicated his steely resolve to his troops. His standing order on Indian raids began: "Commanding officers are expected to continue a pursuit until capture."

had been in the south. Among other things it brought a final and fatal flash of glory to Sheridan's favorite young officer, the extraordinary cavalryman named George Armstrong Custer.

Phil Sheridan and George Custer saw almost everything in similar terms, though Sheridan was more intelligent and much more stable. Yet Custer became the popular hero of the Indian wars. Never a commander of more than a single regiment in the West, he precipitated the best known event of the Indian wars — the battle that proved to be the wars' true climax.

By almost any rational definition, Custer was a fool. He was a bad commander. Most of his men disliked him *(box, page 188)*, distrusted him, feared him — and with good reason. He was personally undisciplined but to those who served under him he was a martinet. His ego was towering and demanded constant feeding. He was emotional in his own strange way, able to kill without a twinge, yet reduced to real tears at a melodrama in the theater. His marriage to the beautiful Elizabeth Bacon was a great love story. She adored him as "the sunshine that lighted my life" and devoted nearly 60 years of widowhood to glorifying his memory.

The son of an Ohio blacksmith, George Custer talked himself into an appointment to West Point where he earned a reputation for slovenliness and a record number of demerits. He graduated into the Civil War, ranked 34th in a class of 34, yet he had a flair that caught the eyes of powerful men. General George McClellan, Commander of the Army, put Custer on his own staff on the basis of a chance meeting. When McClellan was ousted Custer returned to the cavalry and promptly made perhaps the most extraordinary series of leaps in rank in the history of the U.S. Army. Between July 1862 and July 1863 he went from first lieutenant to brigadier general of volunteers and was given command of a brigade of cavalry. In 1865, when Sheridan held command of all the Union cavalry, Custer became a major general and took over one of Sheridan's three divisions. Custer was 25 years old that year.

He cut a splendid figure as a general. One of the Army's finest horsemen, he was a natural athlete who stood just under six feet, had broad shoulders and wore his bright yellow hair in curls that fell to his shoulders. His eyes were vivid blue, startling in an often reddened face, which brightened with emotion or exertion or the sun, since he did not tan. His voice was shrill and at moments of crisis or excitement broke into a stammer — yet it was stirring. He wore a uniform of his own design made of black velveteen with loopings of gold braid that ran up to near the shoulders of his big, puffed sleeves. He carried a heavy straight sword, a trophy he had taken from a Confederate officer whom he shot in the back as he pursued the man through woods; in a letter home he described the killing as "the most exciting sport I ever engaged in."

Contemporary accounts describe him as handsome but in photographs he appears leaden and sometimes even ugly. The photography of his day forced a man to remain still when he sat for a portrait, and in repose the excitement that Custer inspired seemed to disappear. But in person, mounted on a strong horse, his heavy sword held high, his voice like a bugle, the sun flashing on his yellow hair, he seemed to be a man for men to follow. And in sight of the enemy, his instinct was immediate and unswerving: he charged. He did not bother to find out how many troops he was charging, what reserves they might have, what problems of tactics or terrain might develop. He charged.

Rarely did a Custer charge fail: once, in the Civil War, he stormed after Jeb Stuart's forces in the Blue Ridge Mountains; he was surrounded and had to cut his way out with that sword. But otherwise his headstrong tactics generally worked, and Sheridan liked them. When Sheridan pillaged the Shenandoah Valley, Custer led the way. When Sheridan blocked Robert E. Lee's last retreat, it was Custer's division that smashed the Confederate cavalry and turned on Lee's staggering infantry. After Grant and Lee met at Appomattox to end the war, Sheridan paid $20 in gold for the table on which they signed the articles of surrender and presented it to Mrs. Custer with a note saying, "I know of no person more instrumental in bringing about [the surrender] than your most gallant husband."

When the war ended Custer was dropped to the rank of captain. But in 1866, partly because he had attracted the personal attention of President Andrew Johnson, he was given a lieutenant colonelcy in the 7th Cavalry, which was then being formed at Fort Riley, Kansas. Technically he was second-in-command, but the regiment's colonel seemed always to be posted elsewhere on staff duties and Custer was its effective commander for the rest of his life. Partly because of Custer's ferocious discipline and drilling, the men of the 7th became some of the best — and the best known — horse soldiers on the Plains, so that a staff officer, Captain Charles King, would remark in his memoirs that because of the precision of a maneuver, "I knew the 7th Cavalry at a glance."

But Custer was not out to make a reputation simply as a drillmaster. He wanted to be, once more, a spectacular war leader, to become great and famous. He himself explicitly described his craving "to link my name not only to the present but to future generations." In an effort to do so, he began to scramble off on a series of fame-seeking missions that raised serious doubts in the minds of his patrons at headquarters. General Sherman noted in a letter to his brother that Custer had "not too much sense."

Certainly there was something of the boy in his ardent adoration of his pretty wife Libbie. When they were apart Custer wrote her immense flowing letters every night, once dashing off 80 handwritten pages in a single letter. And on post, if Libbie went visiting for

Bundled up against the 20-below-zero cold of a Montana morning, Colonel Miles *(center, in broad-brimmed hat)* briefs his staff before raiding the

the afternoon, George was likely to send an orderly after her, bearing some pointed hint that she had overstayed—perhaps her nightgown or a question about where she might like her trunk to be sent.

The two often romped as children do, running through the house, playing tag, shrieking with laughter. When George had good news to tell, he became so excited that he roared through the house and hurled furniture about. Libbie remembered that she "learned to take up a safe position on top of the table. The most disastrous result of the proceedings was possibly a broken chair, which the master of ceremonies would crash and perhaps throw into the kitchen by way of informing the cook that good news had come."

Despite the glee and smashed furniture that abounded within his own household, Custer tended to be distant to most of his fellow officers. He rarely had anything to do with them socially; at parties, he frequently would retire to his study, dispatching his orderly now and then to invite Libbie to dance alone with him. Like a child, he was given to petulant angers and was shattered by real or fancied slights. Yet he

Sioux in 1877. His careful preparations paid off: outnumbered two to one, his soldiers charged in a blizzard and forced the Indians to surrender.

Flamboyant egotist George A. Custer designed the major general's undress uniform that he wore in this 1865 portrait. It features a sailor-suit collar with a general's stars in each corner and a scarlet cravat.

found it hard to hold a grudge, and usually forgave his enemies—a gesture they rarely returned.

Like a boy, too, he was given to the crudest of practical jokes, often of the kind that involve a bucket of water perched on a half-opened door. One of Custer's favorite tricks on his father was to mount him on a dangerous horse, snatch the aging man's cape over his face to blind him, and lash the horse. In a letter to Libbie he boasted of a more dangerous trick played on his young brother Boston Custer. On a ride across the plains Boston had dismounted to pick a pebble from his horse's hoof. Custer climbed a nearby butte, hid—and then, "I fired my rifle so that the bullet whizzed over his head. When I looked again, 'Bos' was heading his pony toward the command, miles away. I fired another shot in his direction and away 'Bos' flew across the plains." In another letter he ingenuously remarked, "I do not know what we would do without 'Bos' to tease."

The same heedless strain runs through his conduct on campaign. One morning, deep in Indian country and miles from help, Custer abandoned his marching regiment and galloped off to test his staghounds against a herd of antelope. He was completely alone; unlike Crook, he had not the prudence to take an Indian guide or a small hunting party to accompany him.

The chase ran for miles until Custer's attention was diverted to a buffalo—the first he had ever seen, for he was then new to the Plains. The buffalo careered off in another direction and Custer rode beside it, prepared to kill it with his pistol, yet delaying the delicious moment. Finally he steadied his aim, and at that moment the buffalo, as if forewarned, turned to attack Custer's horse. The horse shied. Custer's hand jerked, the pistol fired—and he killed his own horse. The horse fell like a stone, throwing Custer headlong; the buffalo snorted and trotted off. There was the commandant of the 7th Cavalry, alone on foot in hostile Indian country, miles from his regiment, without the faintest idea of where he was or in what direction his regiment lay. Eventually his dogs chose a direction; their master followed them, and after walking for miles saw the regiment's dust on the horizon. End of an afternoon's outing.

The energy, as well as the foolhardiness, of that hunting foray was typical of George Custer. Whenever he went into the field he was a fierce driver, setting a pace that he enjoyed and expected everyone to keep up with.

He could ride a full day without any liquids except for a cup of cold tea or coffee at noon, retain his energy with a minimum of food, fall to the ground and sleep like a dog for an hour or two and spring up refreshed. He often pushed his men through the day and then, while they wearily made camp, would order a fresh horse and ride off to hunt or scout the trail ahead. While everyone around him slept, he sat in his tent writing one of those long letters to Libbie. Men who did not share his frantic energy found his pace cruel, particularly when it was ordered on whim. That he never noticed their suffering was a mark of his egocentricity.

All the while, however, Custer looked to his own comfort. His scouts helped to supply him with fresh game even as his men ate moldy bacon and hardtack. Sometimes he took along a huge iron stove for his tent, and even a woman to cook on it—neither one of much military help to a supposedly mobile column exposed in Indian country. In a series of magazine articles written between 1871 and 1873, Custer complacently describes camping in a blizzard the night before his attack on Black Kettle. He lies in a big tent, warm in his buffalo robes, watching the smoke from his fire drift through the tent flap above. But there is hardly a word of concern for the men who huddled against the snow outside, under shelter halves and wet blankets. Other officers routinely watched over their men; Nelson Miles discussed his plans with them and George Crook would painstakingly check their equipment and supplies. There is no record that such thoughts occurred to Custer.

On another occasion, Custer was leading the 7th Cavalry on a hot, exhausting summertime reconnaissance through Kansas. He was trying to bring Kiowa and Comanche warriors to battle; but the Indians kept skittering beyond the regiment's reach. Finally Custer ordered a desperate march with no precise military objective beyond the wild hope of running into some Indians en route. The regiment blundered 65 miles over alkali flats toward the Platte River; there was not a single break or water hole in the whole stretch. They marched through heat so intense it killed most of the pet dogs that the soldiers often took with them on summer campaigns. At nightfall they were still miles from the river. Custer summoned a handful of officers and several orderlies, and they galloped off, leaving the troops toiling behind. His purpose, Custer later wrote,

A notorious showman, Custer was depicted at center stage by artist Charles Schreyvogel in this painting titled *Custer's Demand*. While General Sheridan *(right rear)* waits with the troops, Custer tells Kiowa war chiefs in sign language that they must go peacefully to a reservation. They went.

was to find a good camping ground. But without further explanation he added that upon reaching the river he had a long, satisfying drink and spread his blankets. He slept so soundly that an Indian raid on a stagecoach station less than a mile away did not wake him. Meanwhile his regiment eventually struck the river three miles below his tent; it was daybreak before all the exhausted, thirsty men reached water.

Besides caring little for his men's welfare on campaign, Custer could become murderous toward them when he felt he had been crossed. He demonstrated the trait right there on the Platte. The 7th always had a high desertion rate, and after that wretched march a number of men slaked their thirst in the river and then simply departed. Custer was furious. That day the column halted at noon, well past the Platte, and a dozen men headed back toward the river, five on foot. Custer ordered the officer of the day to pursue them. Then, his face scarlet, he shouted another order; the pursuing officer was "to bring in none alive." The seven mounted men escaped, but the zealous officer overtook the five on foot and opened fire. One was killed, two were wounded and two survived by pretending to be dead. For the men of the 7th, the incident gave a clear idea of their commander's regard for them.

Eventually the tired and somewhat demoralized 7th pulled into Fort Wallace in western Kansas. Awaiting Custer were the orders of his commanding officer, General W. S. Hancock, to remain in the field, using Fort Wallace as a base and ranging between the Platte and Arkansas rivers. The orders ended explicitly: "The cavalry will be kept constantly engaged."

The man who had ordered deserters shot proceeded to desert his own troops. Claiming that Fort Wallace was low on supplies, Custer readied a column of 75 men to go 150 miles to Fort Hays and 60 more miles on to Fort Harker, the nearest supply dump. The column would return with a wagon train of food and ammunition. But Libbie was at Fort Riley, in eastern Kansas. Custer wanted to see her; so he joined the column, and set a terrible pace.

Some of the men could not keep up; near Downer's Station, where a small detachment of troops was billeted, Indians attacked his rear guard and killed two stragglers. The survivors caught up with the commander and told of the attack, but Custer did not attempt to

What people thought of Custer

After the Battle of the Little Bighorn, a schoolgirl wrote to a New York newspaper: "I enclose ten cents (all I can spare), for a monument to the noble General Custer. He was so young and, as the papers say, so handsome. I could cry tears over his sad fate for such heroes as General Custer are scarce." Her concept of Custer as a flawless hero was the popular one; but among the people who knew him best, opinions *(below)* on the dashing cavalryman were decidedly mixed.

I never met a more enterprising, gallant or dangerous enemy during those four years of terrible war, or a more genial, whole-souled, chivalrous gentleman and friend in peace.
T. L. Rosser, former Major General, Confederate Army

The honor of his country weighed lightly in the scale against the "glorious" name of "Geo. A. Custer," the hardships and danger to his men, as well as the probable loss of life were worthy of but little considerations when dim visions of an "eagle" or even a "star" floated before the excited mind of our Lieut. Colonel.
Theodore Ewert, Private 7th Cavalry

A man respected and beloved by his followers, who would freely follow him into the "jaws of hell."
Mark Kellogg, *New York Herald* correspondent

He was too hard on the men and horses. He changed his mind too often. He was always right. He never conferred enough with his officers. When he got a notion, we had to go.
Jacob Horner, Corporal, 7th Cavalry

He had a very keen sense of his social responsibilities as post commander and believed that our house should be open at all hours to the garrison.
Elizabeth Custer

Some of the officers were friendly and easygoing with their troopers, but Custer struck me as being aloof and removed.
Charles A. Windolf, Sergeant, 7th Cavalry

He was a brave warrior and died a brave man.
Low Dog, veteran of the Battle of the Little Bighorn

I'm only too proud to say that I despised him.
Frederick William Benteen, Captain, 7th Cavalry

punish the Indians or even pause to recover the bodies. He detailed that duty to the men at the station.

The column made the 150 miles to Fort Hays in 55 hours, and arrived with the men and horses exhausted. Custer rode on to Fort Harker accompanied by two officers and two orderlies, making 60 more miles in less than 12 hours. There he roused the commander out of bed, insisted that supplies be sent to the 7th at Fort Wallace, and rushed off to catch a train to Fort Riley, where Libbie awaited him.

This direct disobedience of Hancock's orders was too much even for Custer's high-placed admirers to overlook. In September a court-martial convened to try Custer on no less than seven charges, including not only his disregard of orders but his treatment of the deserters at the Platte. He was convicted on all counts. His punishment was mild enough; explaining that "Gen. Custer's anxiety to see his family at Fort Riley overcame his appreciation of the paramount necessity to obey orders," the court sentenced him to a year's suspension without pay. Yet Phil Sheridan, wielding his lieutenant general's rank to override the court, soon rescued Custer from even that lenient sentence by calling him back to the 7th for a winter campaign.

During that campaign Custer's casual readiness to leave his troops had fatal results when, in November 1868, he attacked Chief Black Kettle's village on the Washita River *(pages 36-38)*. In the course of battle Major Joel Elliot galloped off with 19 men in pursuit of some fleeing Indians. Elliot and his men did not return. Twice during that day a young officer told Custer that he heard heavy firing in the direction Elliot had taken and the detachment was in trouble. Custer paid no heed; he simply gathered his regiment and marched it away without even looking for Elliot.

Weeks later the bodies of Elliot and his men were located within two miles of the battle site. Evidence around the bodies indicated that the men had held out most of the day, and during that day Custer could have rescued them. Custer later explained that he feared attack by other Indians in the vicinity. Yet he had 700 well-armed men, and the Indians showed no signs of attacking him. At this point Custer had something he could portray as a clear-cut victory. Had he risked an Indian counterattack—and a probe after Elliot might have inspired one—his victory could have been con-

verted into an indecisive action. Apparently Custer chose the route to fame and abandoned Elliot; but he never again commanded the loyalty of most of his officers. Years later General David Stanley, who headed an expedition in which the 7th Cavalry took part, described Custer as "a coldblooded, untruthful and unprincipled man," and added that he was "despised" by most of his officers.

The Washita episode also emphasized Custer's fatal weakness in the critical area of tactics. When attacking the village he had divided his force. This was always a high-stakes game. If it worked, the simultaneous charge from several quarters was devastating. But if it failed, each unit could be surrounded and destroyed. Even more important, Custer attacked without reconnoitering. He had never forgotten the success of those blind, smashing attacks of the Civil War. And now, because he did not order reconnaissance, he did not know that there were other Indian encampments near Black Kettle's, or how many warriors these camps contained.

Custer never bothered to reassess his tactics, and thus overcome such tragic shortcomings. Moreover, he was fast running out of time. During the next two years the 7th saw no action at all on the Plains. Then in 1873 it formed part of an expedition seeking a northern railway route through Dakota and Montana. Here, Custer led his men into a battle with Sioux warriors who fled so quickly they may have given Custer a dangerously scornful view of their fighting talents. In 1873 Custer was posted to Fort Abraham Lincoln in the Dakotas, where he was to command a reconnaissance into the Black Hills *(pages 200-201)*. At the fort, Sioux raiders drove off his herd of mules and he galloped after them with such haste that his troopers were strung along the prairie for miles. In his haste, he left the fort totally defenseless; Libbie Custer, who had come to live at the post, never forgot the terror she and the other women at Abraham Lincoln felt that day.

Altogether, Custer's abortive fights provided little promise for his competence in real combat. Yet the combat came. Late in the fall of 1875, Phil Sheridan drew up plans for a climactic campaign on the northern Plains, involving the same sort of fighting that Miles had done so successfully in Texas. By the spring of 1876 the northern campaign really got moving. And then, as it turned out, the fighting would lead to a disaster.

With his bride Libbie, Custer poses for a
Mathew Brady portrait. Soon after his marriage he asked her to join him at camp. She
wrote in reply, "I love luxury, dress, comfort. But, how gladly I will give them up!"

The private life of "The Boy General"

A Civil War general at 23 (the nation's press dubbed him "The Boy General") George Custer never adopted the life habits of the hardbitten professional soldiers around him. Instead, he made himself the kingpin of a warm domestic circle whose recreations included musicales and amateur theatricals as well as hunting and riding.

In 1864 Custer married Elizabeth Bacon, the prettiest girl in Monroe, Michigan, where both of them had lived as children. After the wedding, except when he was on campaign he kept his Libbie at his side literally, if possible: even when they had a meal alone together they would sit side by side rather than at opposite ends of the table.

But there was a paradox: possessive though he was with his wife, Custer himself may not have been above dalliance. After the Battle of the Washita, he made a captive Indian girl his mistress, and a Cheyenne scout claimed that even on the way to Little Bighorn, Custer had his mind on richly dressed Indian maidens: "When we get there," Custer reportedly jested, "I'm going to find the girl with the most elk teeth on her dress and take her with me."

The Custers had no children. Instead they had pets. Custer tamed and prized an extraordinary range of animals, from a mouse that ran playfully through his abundant hair to a wolf that tore the sheets off his clothesline. At one time he had a pack of 40 dogs and he spoiled them all outrageously. For Libbie, the dogs were not so much pets as trials. When the Custers moved from one post to another, if the dogs got tired George would insist on piling them into her wagon. When the caravan stopped to eat, the animals had to be beaten away from the food with sticks. And at night, Libbie shared her tent with the whole pack. "If I secured a place in the bed," she wrote, "I was fortunate."

At Fort Abraham Lincoln in the Dakotas, Custer characteristically surrounds himself with family and friends for the photographer. He sits at center with a visibly aged Libbie at his right, while on the step above are a family friend, brother-in-law James Calhoun and Custer's sister Margaret. Another brother-in-law, Fred Calhoun, is just below Custer, and a second friend is at the far right.

Custer's home at Fort Abraham Lincoln boasted five chimneys and a complex heating plant. To keep it warm he reprieved a soldier arrested for drunkenness and put him to work stoking fires around the clock.

An attentive Custer turns pages for his sister Margaret, whose piano playing has apparently mesmerized Mrs. Custer *(center)* and their guests. A music lover who could whistle the arias of an opera after hearing them once, Custer found it infuriating when members of his entourage drummed on the piano until it finally went out of tune.

Seated below his own portrait, Custer pens a manuscript; the portrait above his wife is of his patron, General Philip Sheridan. Custer insisted that Libbie stay by him while he composed—which gave rise to a rumor, denied by her, that she wrote part of his *War Memoirs*.

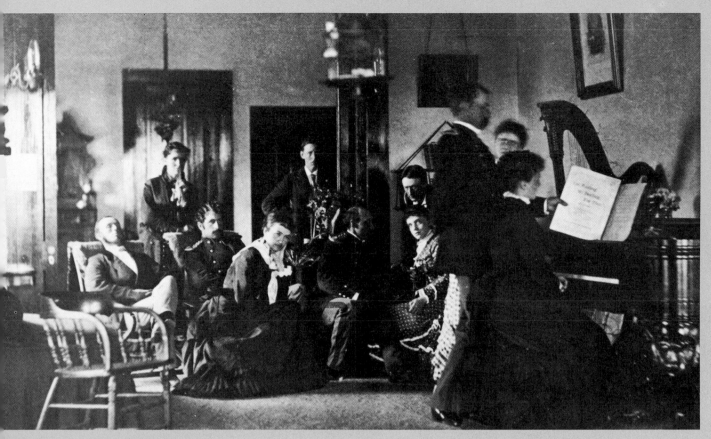

Impersonating a Sioux chief in an amateur playlet, thespian Custer examines the headdress of his "bride," played by a friend of Mrs. Custer's. He took his acting seriously, and once wrote, "I wish we had someone competent to give us lessons in private theatricals."

This richly framed photo of Custer and friend in Texas in 1865 was a family souvenir.

Natty in a tailored buckskin jacket, a costume he also wore en route to the battle of the Little Bighorn, Custer (center, with Libbie at his right) cuts a striking figure on an 1875 outing in Dakota. Adored by women everywhere, he presented admirers with locks of his hair.

An ardent hunter, Custer sent Libbie this picture of himself and his first grizzly, along with an Indian scout and two soldiers, from Dakota Territory in 1874. In an accompanying letter he exulted, "I have reached the height of a hunter's fame." On campaign he would stay up nights, preparing trophy heads of freshly killed animals.

On a Kansas plain, Custer relaxes with three of his hounds. Partly visible at far right is a pelican he captured on the Arkansas River in 1868. He kept it as a pet for a while, then sent it East to an Audubon Society aviary. The only other animal he gave up voluntarily was a wildcat that Libbie finally made him send to a zoo.

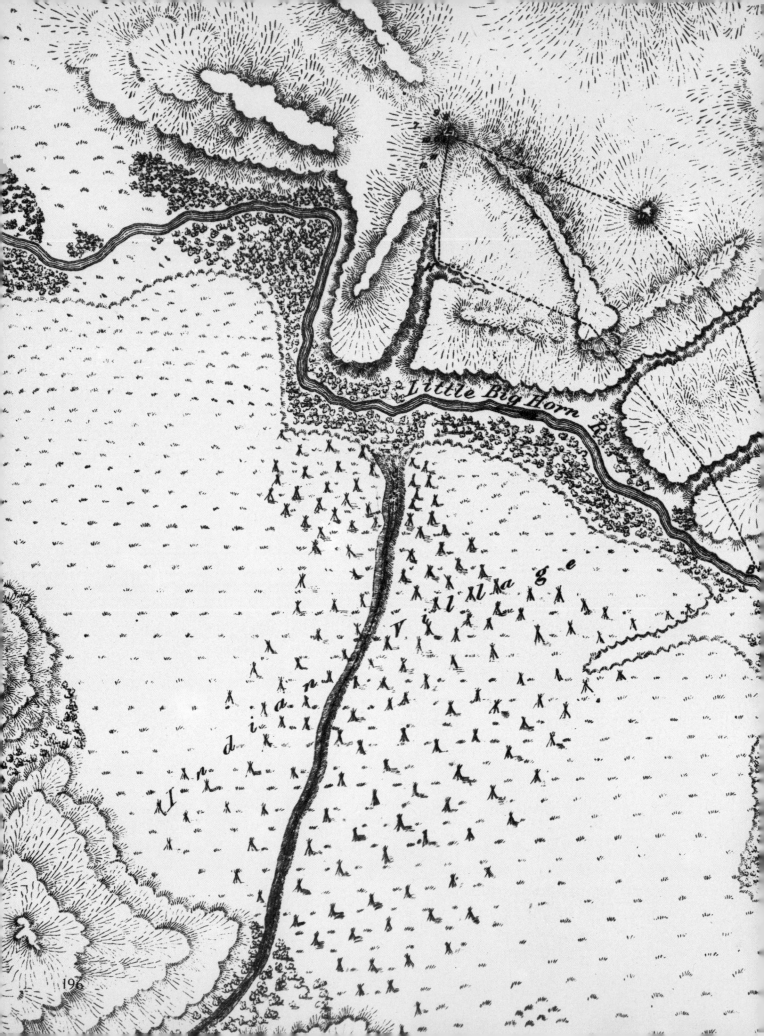

Little Big Horn R.

Indian village

196

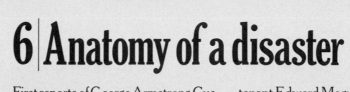

6|Anatomy of a disaster

First reports of George Armstrong Custer's crushing defeat on the Little Bighorn River were ignored by his superior officer, General Alfred H. Terry. Hurrying upriver to meet Custer, Terry could not believe "that disaster could have overtaken so large a force." A day and a half later a stunned Terry stood on the riverbank amid the debris of a hastily abandoned Indian encampment and viewed the grisly evidence for himself. Strewn over half a square mile of ravines and rises lay the bodies of more than 200 men, all that was left of Custer and five companies of the 7th Cavalry Regiment.

Anticipating a formal investigation, Terry ordered his staff engineer, Lieu-tenant Edward Maguire, to prepare the map reproduced on these pages. It shows the sinuous course of the river, flanked on one side by high bluffs and on the other by the flat grasslands on which Sioux and Cheyenne Indians had pitched their camp. Dotted lines on the north bank of the river lead to the field where Custer died.

The trail, Terry reported, "turns upon itself, almost completes a circle and ceases. It is marked by the remains of officers and men."

From the evidence Terry gathered immediately after the battle, what had happened seemed obvious — but after years of analysis and reconstruction, men would still ponder how and why.

From battlefield evidence, Army cartographers traced Custer's last maneuvers.

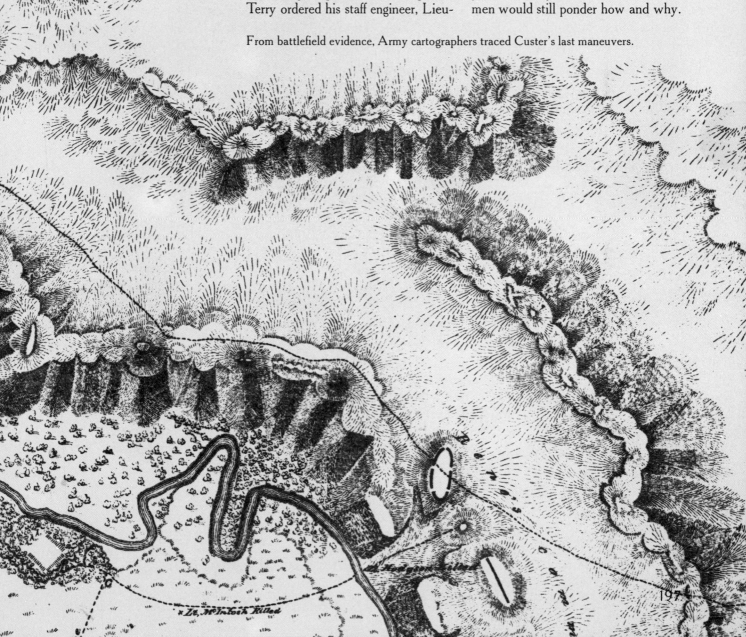

Lt. McIntosh Killed

Little Bighorn: "Indians enough for all of us"

The brass trumpets of the 7th U.S. Cavalry rang out in the thin, clear air, and the regiment's 12 companies went on parade. Proudly, in perfect columns of four, some 600 mounted men wheeled, lined up and saluted a group of officers that included Alfred Terry, their commanding general. The time was noon, on the 22nd of June, 1876; the place was eastern Montana where Rosebud Creek runs into the Yellowstone River. On the bank of the Yellowstone the sternwheeler *Far West* rode at its mooring. Otherwise, the region was a wilderness, without evidence of humanity save what the soldiers themselves had brought in.

At General Terry's side was the commanding officer of the regiment, Lieutenant Colonel George Armstrong Custer, his yellow hair newly trimmed, wearing his buckskins, a white wide-brimmed hat and high boots. While the men of the 7th rode past him, Custer curbed his prancing sorrel gelding, Vic, one of the strongest, fastest horses in the Army. Then, the last salute executed, the last notes of the trumpets dying in the wilderness quiet, the 7th moved out, riding south toward the headwaters of the Rosebud. Custer tarried a moment, talking and watching his troops.

Colonel John Gibbon called out to him: "Now, don't be greedy, Custer, as there are Indians enough for all of us. Wait for us." Custer looked up, his face red, his

> *I am not impetuous or impulsive. I resent that. Everything that I have ever done has been the result of the study that I have made of imaginary military situations that might arise. When I became engaged in campaign or battle and a great emergency arose, everything that I had ever read or studied focused in my mind as if the situation were under a magnifying glass and my decision was the instantaneous result.*
>
> — George Armstrong Custer

eyes that startling blue. "No," he called gaily, waving, his stutter coming up suddenly, "I-I won't!" What did he mean? No one knew exactly, or would ever know; in the next moment he lifted the reins and Vic broke into a canter, carrying the 7th's commander to the head of his regiment.

Thus it was that George Custer set out on the campaign that was to bring him immortality at last, though hardly of the kind he sought. The battle he was heading into would turn out to be the single most important engagement of the Indian wars, and one of the most discussed and pondered and analyzed in all U.S. history. Setting a brutal pace, Custer rode for the valley of the Little Bighorn River.

The 7th Cavalry made 12 miles up the valley of Rosebud Creek on the 22nd, and stopped for the night at some of the last rich pasture they would find for their horses. The men unsaddled, rubbed their horses down and started small cooking fires. At dusk the trumpeter sounded officers' call. Gathering at Custer's tent, the officers found their commander in a strange mood, nervous, tense, irritable. He fussily enumerated a list of marching orders—no trumpet calls except in emergencies; orders would be cleared with him personally; and only he would select campsites or decide when to break camp. He went into great detail about why he had refused the offer of an extra battalion of cavalry and a battery of Gatling guns: the men of the 7th, he said, could handle any force they met, and the guns would only slow them down. He appealed to them to share his pride in the regiment. The whole performance—the instructions, the explanations, the appeals—was an odd

In an idealized portrait, George Armstrong Custer wears a tailored jacket and gauntlets of buckskin and sports the stars of a major general, his brevet rank in the Civil War.

one; for the self-assured Custer, it was astonishing. A junior officer observed to a friend later that night: "I believe General Custer is going to be killed, because I have never heard Custer talk in that way before."

They understood that Custer was under unusual pressure. Some of the pressure was internal and psychological—no one knows how dangerous and critical Custer may have seen his own personal position to be. But there was more than enough pressure in the military situation itself. This had started to develop the previous year, when General Philip Sheridan had decided to crush the Indians on the northern Plains. The object of his plans was the Sioux, the most numerous and warlike of all Indian tribes on the northern Plains, backed in 1875 by some of the northern Cheyennes. Many of the Sioux had been infuriated when hordes of miners and settlers invaded their reservation in the Black Hills (right). Now Indians clustered in great numbers, ever more warlike, in eastern Montana and Wyoming, where the plains become mountains.

Sheridan's plans were simple. General George Crook would lead a column north to Montana from Fort Fetterman, in Wyoming. Colonel Gibbon would bring a column east from Fort Ellis, in Montana. And a column led by Custer would drive westward from Fort Abraham Lincoln in Dakota Territory (map, page 206). The Indians would be caught by one column or another, and their power would be permanently broken, for Sheridan believed that any one of his columns could crush any conceivable Indian resistance.

While these plans were developing, Custer and his pretty wife Libbie, apparently having found Fort Abraham Lincoln in winterbound Dakota too dull, were in New York City. During the early fall of 1875 Custer had taken off on an extended leave, and he and Libbie were savoring the delights of the big city. They went to a gay round of parties and dinners and plays. Custer addressed both the Century Society and The New-York Historical Society and agreed to give a series of lectures in 1876. He demonstrated anew his ability to charm important men, among them James Gordon Bennett, publisher of the powerful *New York Herald*.

In part at Bennett's instigation a national political scandal was brewing, and Custer came to play an important—and, in terms of his career, potentially dangerous—role. The fact that 1876 was a Presidential

A trumped-up gold strike in Dakota

Two years before his death George Custer led an expedition that helped to bring on the battle of the Little Bighorn. In the summer of 1874, Custer's 7th Cavalry was ordered into the Black Hills, the most remote part of the Sioux reservation in western Dakota. Officially, the Army sent the expedition to make a reconnaissance with the objective of establishing a military post there. But in the background lay another and a very different objective for white America—gold.

For decades explorers and prospectors had been spreading rumors of gold in the Black Hills. Frontiersmen were hoping for confirmation. When Custer's expedition was announced, every Westerner expected him to find gold and to tell the world about it. The flamboyant glory-hunter did not let them down.

The 7th pulled out of Fort Lincoln, near Bismarck, with an entourage that included two prospectors and three newspaper correspondents. Custer met no resistance from the Sioux; most of the tribes were in Montana for their usual summer reunion. But he did find gold—though only minute quantities. Nevertheless, Custer indicated in a report that gold was in fact plentiful; his prospectors, he said, had "found gold among the roots of the grass." Newspapers sounded the call: *"Prepare For Lively Times!"* trumpeted a headline in the Yankton *Press and Dakotaian*. "The National Debt to be Paid When Custer Returns."

The lively times were not long in coming. A stampede of gold-hungry miners thundered into the Black Hills. More than a thousand white men squatted on the Indian lands, trespassing upon their sacred places and disrupting their ways of life. For two years, many of the Sioux remained willing to negotiate. But in the end, harried, pressed and finally attacked by Custer, they turned to their weapons—and slaughtered him.

Custer's 110 wagons snake their way through the Black Hills' Castle Creek Valley. The region promised wealth not only in gold but also in timber, game and grazing lands.

election year made the scandal especially juicy. Democrats charged that W. W. Belknap, Secretary of War to Republican President Ulysses S. Grant, was profiteering in the revenues of traders at Army posts; the traders, according to the accusations, cheated soldiers and Indians alike to make fortunes, part of which they funneled back to Belknap. Though Belknap quickly resigned as soon as the scandal began to break, the Democrats pressed an impeachment trial before the Senate. Custer himself had had trouble with the post trader at Fort Abraham Lincoln, who had imposed outrageous prices on the men of the 7th. When Custer brought the matter to Belknap's attention, the Secretary had found for the trader and had thus earned Custer's permanent hatred. Then, when the scandal over Belknap broke, Custer helped to fan its flames; he offered to give evidence against Belknap, and he was probably the author of at least one of the more devastating articles that ran in Bennett's newspaper. Naturally, he was summoned to Washington to testify before Congress.

But now he faced a dilemma. The call to Washington came in March 1876—at a time when he should have stayed in Dakota, readying his regiment for a campaign that was particularly important to him. In the 1876 fighting on the northern Plains, Custer expected to regain some of the national fame he had won during the Civil War, and afterward by his slaughter of Indians on the Washita. It had been eight years since the boy general had reaped glory in combat on the Washita and it was time to renew the glow. Chafing to return to the West, Custer appeared before the committee and proved himself more righteous than wise. He offered a mass of hearsay evidence against Belknap—evidence he could not hope to prove—and on equally flimsy grounds he accused President Grant's brother, Orville Grant, of influence-peddling and receiving payoffs. The testimony did not endear him to the President.

Custer had now blundered into a morass. After the Congressional hearings he was summoned to testify at the trial. He won release from that duty—but Grant ordered that another officer lead the Dakota column against the Indians. Custer went to the White House hat in hand and sat in an anteroom for hours waiting to plead his cause; Grant would not see him.

Custer was frantic; the chance of a lifetime was ebbing away. With a new scandal in the air, the Democratic Party scented an opportunity for their first Presidential victory since the ending of the Civil War. To carry it off, the Democrats would need a strong candidate, popular, well known—a war hero, perhaps. These things are never discussed openly in politics, but Custer may have been led to believe that with a fresh victory behind him to splash his name once more over the nation's newspapers, he could be that candidate.

At last, driven to desperation, Custer fled Washington without orders. Under instructions from the Commander of the Army, William Sherman, General Sheridan had an aide meet Custer's train at Chicago to place him under arrest. With Sheridan's permission, Custer sent telegrams to Sherman pleading his case. He never got an answer. Then he turned to General Alfred Terry, who had been named by Sheridan to lead the Dakota column. At a meeting in St. Paul, Minnesota, he is said to have knelt on the floor before Terry in tears as he pleaded with him to intercede. Terry did so, perhaps out of pity, perhaps out of natural decency —or perhaps because he himself had no battle experience against Indians and felt he needed a relatively knowledgeable commander like Custer.

With Terry's help, Custer composed a penitent telegram to Grant asking, as one soldier to another, not that he be allowed to lead the expedition, but that he be spared the ignominy of having his men go into combat without him. Terry forwarded the telegram with a message of his own, saying that he would lead the command and adding that Custer would be "very valuable with his regiment." Sheridan endorsed the plea and Grant relented. Within a few hours of his reprieve, Custer reportedly told other officers that he would find a way to "cut loose" and "swing clear" of Terry and run on his own. Custer did one other thing: against Sherman's specific orders, he permitted Mark Kellogg, a reporter for Bennett's New York Herald, to march with the 7th. The obligations of gratitude would have to bow to the need for publicity.

As planned, Gibbon came from the west, Terry and Custer from the east; when they met on the Yellowstone, Terry took control of both columns. There was no liaison between Terry and Crook, who was supposed to be working his way north from Wyoming. Neither was there any serious attempt to determine the Indians' numbers; instead, the Dakota column scouted

George A. Custer U.S.A. Having
this day made application to
the New York Life In Co for a
Life insurance Policy of Five
Thousand Dollars, and he having
paid me the Sum of One Hundred
and Twenty Seven 80/100 Dollars premium
on Same. I hereby on behalf of said
Company do insure the life of the
Said Geo. A. Custer from this date
provided that said application
is accepted at the Home office in
New York, and in the Event of the
Company declining to accept Same
to return all premium paid on account
of said policy to me
    Dated 25th May 1874 at
Fort A. Lincoln D.T.

        J. W. Riddle
        Manager Genl Agent
        New York Life —

Note for $127 80/100 payable
on Oct 1st at Dawson & Co
banking house St Paul.
        G. A. C.

the rivers it crossed as it moved toward the rendezvous. Many rivers of that country run north, roughly parallel to one another. The Powder, the Tongue and the Bighorn (of which the Little Bighorn is a tributary) empty into the Yellowstone, which in turn empties into the Missouri. And about June 14 a 7th Cavalry scouting party led by Major Marcus A. Reno had found a heavy Indian trail going up Rosebud Creek, between the Tongue and Bighorn rivers.

What no one in the Army knew was that the Indians would fight with a force they had never mustered before and could never muster again. The battle that lay ahead was often to be called Custer's Last Stand. In fact, it was also the Indians' last stand. Camped on the Little Bighorn was one of the greatest concentrations of Indians ever gathered on the North American continent. They may have numbered as many as 12,000, with at least 1,500 to 2,500 warriors. Even more important, many of them were going to fight not in their usual individual fashion, but as a striking force of cavalry. In fact, they had already begun to fight in this fashion. The soldiers of Terry's columns did not know it, but on June 17, five days before the 7th marched, the Indians had engaged Crook on the upper Rosebud and had sent him reeling back to Wyoming.

Ignorant of everything except the Indians' approximate location, which had been deduced from Reno's scouting report, Terry divided his forces. Custer would take the 7th up the Rosebud to follow the trail Reno had found. Terry expected the trail to turn westward from the Rosebud and cross over the divide to the valley of the Little Bighorn. To complete Terry's plan, he and Gibbon would go up the Yellowstone to the mouth of the Bighorn, and up that river to the Little Bighorn. There, the Gibbon and Custer columns would be in position to trap the Indians between them.

The entire plan was predicated on a single powerful conviction: that the Indians would flee when attacked. They usually had in the past, fighting mainly in guerrilla fashion, running, striking and running again. For years, these same officers had been frustrated repeatedly by Indians who hit settlers' farms and stagecoach stations, then vanished when the punishing Army arrived. With Custer the conviction that no Indian would ever stand and fight had become an obsession. Give the Indians a chance to escape and they would take it, scat-

tering like rabbits or field mice. And with them would go the victory for which he now was desperate.

For Custer, at this moment in his life, everything rested on immediate success. He was gambling not only an uncertain future in politics, but his Army career itself. Only a towering public reputation can protect an officer from the sort of Presidential displeasure Custer had provoked. Without some new military accomplishment he was probably finished — and the ruin of his career would have been the equivalent of death for Custer.

The assumption that the Indians would attempt to flee was behind Terry's instructions to Custer. Everyone agreed that the Indians' best chance of escape was to head south to the Big Horn Mountains; there, split into small groups, they would be hard to find. Custer was not to rush to the attack, but was to block their escape route. Terry's instructions were clear, and though he phrased them courteously and left open the usual possibility of change if the situation changed, they were intended as orders. But they were issued to an officer who was often insubordinate, whose ego was immense and who believed that success always lay in striking hard and immediately. Terry must have suspected at least that when Custer found Indians he would hit them, without regard to orders. Colonel Gibbon certainly suspected it — which explains his half-joking remonstrance to Custer that morning: Don't be greedy.

Thus it was that George Custer came to that curious officers' call that night on the Rosebud. One of his most fundamental and dangerous weaknesses was evident at that meeting. Ever since he had abandoned Major Joel Elliott and 19 men on the Washita River in 1868, he had been unable to command the respect and loyalty of all his officers. Soon after the Washita affair, one of them had written a letter to a friend angrily accusing Custer of cowardice. The letter was published anonymously in a newspaper, the *Missouri Democrat,* and Custer was livid: obviously an officer in the regiment had written it. Custer summoned his officers and, with the newspaper in one hand and a dog whip twitching in the other, promised to thrash the man who had written it if his identity ever emerged. Captain Frederick W. Benteen, the regiment's senior captain with the brevet rank of colonel, six years older than Custer, and a particular friend of Elliott's, glanced at the newspaper. He said coolly, addressing Custer by the brevet

The sternwheeler *Far West* was a key performer in the final act of Custer's life. The boat supplied his troops, was the scene of the prebattle strategy session and brought wounded men downstream after the battle.

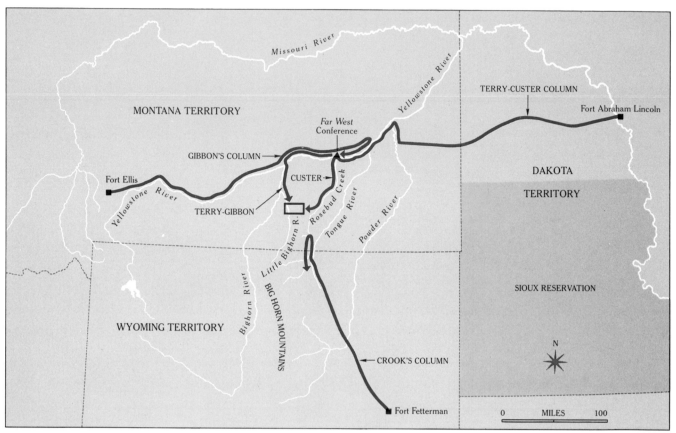

THE PRELUDE TO CATASTROPHE was General Philip Sheridan's three-pronged offensive against the Sioux. In 1876, Sheridan sent separate columns converging on Indians in the Powder River region. One column was led by General George Crook, one by Colonel John Gibbon, and one by General Alfred Terry, whose lieutenant colonel was George Custer. An Indian force turned Crook back on Rosebud Creek. Meanwhile, aboard the steamer *Far West*, Terry formed a plan to join Gibbon's column and move south to a Sioux camp on the Little Bighorn. To block the Indians' escape route Custer was told to ride to the Rosebud headwaters, then north; instead, he followed an Indian trail leading toward the Little Bighorn and the battleground shown opposite.

rank he had held in the Civil War: "If there's to be a whipping, General, you can start in. I wrote that letter." His bluff called, Custer flushed and barked, "Colonel Benteen, I shall see you later, sir," then hurried away. The matter was never mentioned again.

As far as possible, Custer surrounded himself with approving officers and with his own family. His brother Captain Tom Custer, and his brother-in-law, Lieutenant James Calhoun, were members of the regiment; another brother, Boston Custer, and a nephew, Armstrong Reed, came along on this campaign as civilians. But Custer was estranged from most of his officers.

Now, at the officers' call, Custer returned to the old sore subject of loyalty. Some of his officers, he re-minded his staff, had gone to headquarters to criticize his conduct. He was willing to hear complaints, he said, but they should be made within the regiment; now, as never before, he needed his subordinates' backing. Again, it was the crusty Benteen who challenged his commander. Would he care to be specific, Benteen asked, as to who was at fault? Custer reddened. "I am not here to be catechised by you," he snapped, "but for your own information, I will state that none of my remarks have been directed towards you." With that he dismissed them. It was a lame beginning for a major campaign and everyone knew it.

They were marching by 5:00 on the morning of the 23rd and Custer set an awful pace. The sun climbed

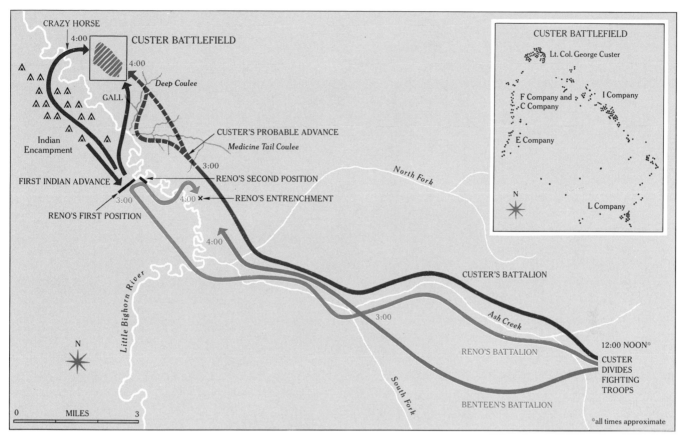

THE FATAL DECISION that precipitated disaster was Custer's order to divide his force. Having found the Sioux encampment, he sent one battalion, under Captain Frederick Benteen, to scout the hills to the west. Another, under Major Marcus Reno, was dispatched to the southern end of the encampment, while Custer himself rode on to attack from the north. Reno was soon turned from his first position in the valley, and retreated to a second. Finally he fled across the Little Bighorn to a bluff, to be joined by Benteen, who had come back after finding no Indians. As for Custer, he headed into Medicine Tail Coulee. He and his five companies were then forced up some hills away from the river, and there annihilated. The inset shows the positions in which they fell.

high, the air dried and the heat grew more intense. Slowly the column stretched out, stragglers dropping so far behind that they eventually arrived in camp hours after the leaders. The hard riding caused blisters to form and then split on men's legs, and horses began to suffer from sores caused by the sweat under the saddles. In some parts of the Indian trail they were following, the ground was cut to powder six inches deep. Alkaline dust clouded around the suffering troopers, burning their eyes and throats. Swarming buffalo gnats, tiny as dust particles, stung and swelled their eyelids. Deerflies tortured the exhausted horses.

The Indian trail was awesomely big and clear. Another joined it; from that point on, the ground was so rutted by lodgepoles dragged by Indian ponies as to resemble a plowed field. The grass all around was cropped to the roots; the huge Indian herds that had gone by had left perilously little fodder for the exhausted cavalry horses and mules.

On the second day of the march, the soldiers passed one deserted campsite after another in quick succession. It seemed to them that individual bands of Indians must have been moving very slowly, a mile or two at a time. But the scouts knew that what they were seeing was not a series of camps, but a single camp made by a group so huge that its individual camp circles had stretched for miles, like beads strung along the creek. They came to a great camp circle where a framework of

207

Scout Mitch Bouyer warned Custer—in vain—that the Little Bighorn valley held more Indians than the cavalry could handle. Bouyer then sent other scouts to the rear—and went on to die with Custer.

lodgepoles still in place showed that a great sun dance had been held. Custer had no way of knowing it, but at this point about three weeks earlier Chief Sitting Bull had had a vision of soldiers falling into his camp, signifying that they would attack and be killed.

At first the pony droppings had been dry, but as the command moved along, the droppings became fresher. The men began to notice the remains of fires so recent that ashes still flew in the wind, and roasted buffalo ribs, though gnawed clean, had not yet dried.

With their strung-out horses laboring along the ever-freshening trail, the troopers went more than 30 miles over hard terrain on June 23rd and about 28 miles on the 24th before they stopped at sundown on the upper reaches of Rosebud Creek. Their camp lay in the lee of a high bluff where little grass had been left by the Indian ponies and there were splashes of wild-rose bushes in vivid bloom. Fireflies flickered along the river and owls fell on their night prey. But the exhausted men had no eyes for beauty as they straggled in on their sore-footed, stumbling mounts. They ate and slept in their clothes, for they knew that they might be making a night march. Custer had sent three of his Crow Indian scouts ahead to follow the Indian trail. At about 9 p.m. they returned: as expected, the trail had turned westward to cross the divide between the Rosebud and the valley of the Little Bighorn.

From the beginning, all the scouts, white men as well as the Arikaras and the Crows, had understood the meaning of the huge trail they were following, and they had become increasingly gloomy. On the first night out the half-breed scout Mitch Bouyer, who had roamed this country for 30 years, asked a young officer if he had ever fought the Sioux. When the youngster confidently answered that the 7th could handle them, Bouyer said, "Well, I can tell you we are going to have a damned big fight."

Lonesome Charley Reynolds, who two years earlier had carried out Custer's report of gold in the Black Hills, had scouted the region during the winter and early spring. The Indians had been gathering guns for months, he told Terry and Custer, and every move they made indicated that they intended to fight. An infected finger on Reynolds' gun hand was so painful he carried the hand in a sling, and his feeling about this campaign matched the feeling in his hand. Twice he

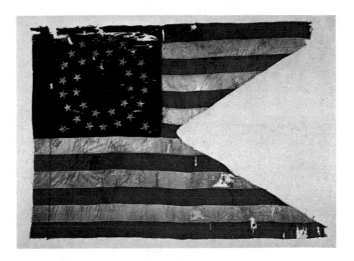

had asked Terry to relieve him; each time Terry had shamed him into staying.

The scouts had spent their lives tracking animals and men. They reacted to a broken twig, a grass stem pressed in the wrong direction, a single moccasin track. Now they were following a trail that in places spread more than a half-mile wide, leaving the ground broken as by a cattle drive. They knew there was more than one trail to this gathering, that it must involve several tribes of Sioux, as well as the northern Cheyennes. They felt certain that there would be more of the enemy than anyone had ever seen together at one time.

Custer's favorite scout warned him in plain language of what lay ahead. Bloody Knife was an Arikara, a mature man who wore the white man's shirt and pants but held his long gray hair in place with a strip of bright red flannel. The Crow and Arikara scouts, commanded by another Custer favorite, Lieutenant Charles Varnum, were enemies of the Sioux. The Arikaras had been disturbed by bad signs on this campaign: by unusually high water in the streams, by a freak snowstorm three weeks earlier, and now by the terrifying size of this trail. While the regiment was still at the Yellowstone, they had ridden in a somber circle singing their death songs. At some stops along the trail they had engaged in rites seeking the protection of the spirits. Later, Bloody Knife himself approached Custer and announced that there were more Sioux ahead than there were bullets in the belts of the soldiers.

It was a more accurate forecast than anyone knew; even the pessimistic scouts did not expect to find 2,000

209

or more Indian warriors awaiting Custer's 600 men.

Custer must have known that the force ahead was huge. But he rejected the scouts' warnings that the odds against him would be overwhelming; instead, he fretted at the possibility that the Indians might get away from him. He was supremely confident of the 7th's capacity to defeat any Indians it met, and indeed, the great size of the Indian force appears to have made him all the more eager for a fight. The greater the number he defeated, after all, the greater would be the scope and the fame of his victory.

Accordingly, he instructed his troops to prepare to march again at 11 p.m. In doing so, he was clearly disobeying the instructions that he himself had received. Terry had told him to swing well to the south, then double back to prevent any possibility of an Indian escape. Instead, Custer had pushed his command at such brutal speed that he was far beyond the point that Terry would have expected him to reach. Now he prepared to attack immediately on his own. Waiting for Terry and Gibbon to come up the Little Bighorn from the other side would have meant sharing the victory. Continuing south as he had been instructed to do would have risked a meeting with Crook's column (no one knew that Crook was already back in Wyoming)—and that would have reduced Custer to a subordinate again and made the victory Crook's.

So Custer started his exhausted men and their exhausted horses on a night march of 10 miles up the divide between the Rosebud and the Little Bighorn. The stars were bright above but the dust rose in furry clouds about them. The men felt their way, listening to the clink of mess cups in the unit ahead, knowing when they passed out of the dust that they had lost the trail, and turning back into the choking cloud, their horses jamming into each other and those of the troop behind, horses kicking, biting, neighing, men cursing and kicking at each other's mounts, the whole column backing and colliding on the steep path. And now and then the thirsty, tired, mean-tempered mules brayed clear as trumpet calls in the night, advertising for miles the presence of a marching army.

At 2 a.m. the head of the column reached a deep, wooded ravine. It was hours before the whole regiment caught up and stopped. The water in the ravine was too alkaline to drink; the horses snorted and reared back in mistrust when they approached it. Some of the men unsaddled and rubbed their horses' lathered backs with dry grass and dust, but many merely wrapped their horses' reins around their arms and fell to the ground to sleep. Then, six hours later, the troops took up their march again. After 10 more grueling miles, they stopped in another wooded ravine, just below the crest of the divide.

The noise and the clouds of dust towering over the moving column had provided clear signs of the soldiers' presence. But none of this mattered, for Sioux scouts had had the regiment under observation for some time. The soldiers themselves knew this to some extent, for their Indian scouts had reported seeing fresh Sioux tracks on several occasions, and one claimed he had even been close enough to a Sioux to converse with him in the universal sign language of the Plains. The only advantage Custer had, then, was the speed of his movement gained from the night march. Afterward, all authorities agreed that once he turned off the Rosebud he was committed, orders or not, to attack. His decision to make that turn rather than continue south was the crucial move that led to battle.

During the previous night Custer had sent Lieutenant Varnum and a party of scouts ahead to a knob later called the Crow's Nest, perched high on the divide; from that lookout point they could see the valley of the Little Bighorn about 15 miles away. Varnum had not slept for some 36 hours; during those hours he had ridden more than 60 miles on constant probes away from the main column. While waiting for the dawn to touch the east, he napped for 45 minutes. The others watched the valley unfold in the light. Despite all their expectations, what they saw astonished them.

The Little Bighorn is a smallish river, running cold and clear in horseshoe bends through a broad valley. On the eastern side, from which the scouts were looking, the river cuts against steep bluffs 80 to 100 feet high. On the western side lies a flat plain, in some places as much as two miles wide. In the growing light, while Varnum slept, the scouts began to sense that the hills beyond the flat, about 20 miles from where they watched, looked wrong somehow. And then they realized that they were looking at horses. Numbering 20,000 or more, horses covered the hills like a brownish carpet in the distance. The scouts agreed that it was the greatest pony herd they had ever seen. They awakened Varnum. His eyes blurred by sleep, he could not find what they pointed out. Look for the horses, they urged, "like worms crawling in the grass," and though Varnum still couldn't see them, he trusted the scouts' eyes better than his own. At 5 a.m., with the light brightening, he sent word back to Custer.

When the message arrived, Custer rode through the camp issuing orders. He was wearing a clean blue flannel shirt, buckskin trousers tucked into long boots, his broad-brimmed white hat and a brace of pistols. Soon the troops moved out at a steady walk, and after more than an hour they reached a wooded pocket just below the Crow's Nest. They waited there as Custer rode on to the observation point. The sun was climbing and already the day promised to be scorching.

When Custer reached the Crow's Nest the valley was hazy; even with glasses he could not make out the horses that the scouts had seen in the clarity of early morning with the sun at their backs. Bouyer told him it was the biggest village he had ever encountered in his three decades among these Indians. But if anything is clear about Custer at that moment, it is the fact that he did not care how big the village was. Bloody Knife and Custer were friends; earlier that morning Bloody Knife had warned him: "We'll find enough Sioux to keep fighting two or three days." Custer had smiled. "Oh, I guess we'll get through with them in one day," he had said. On the night before, Lonesome Charley Reynolds had given his few possessions to his friends, implying that he did not expect to survive the next day.

A century later, the inability of Custer, that sharp-eyed huntsman, to see the enemy seems puzzling, al-

most suspect. Perhaps he simply was not prepared to admit the danger of his position. The night before, he had told several officers that they were going into the fight of their lives; to others he had said, "The largest Indian camp on the North American continent is ahead and I am going to attack it." Custer was famous for his luck. He relied on it. The things he said and did suggest that he now considered the presence of so many Indians the greatest luck of all.

He returned to the regiment, but Varnum, still at his post on the Crow's Nest, saw something that had a critical effect on the situation. A group of Indians was moving downstream. Varnum assumed that the most humiliating possibility was being realized—the Indians were starting to escape. He sent a runner galloping after Custer. In fact, this small group of Indians was hurrying to the main camp for safety after sighting the soldiers; in doing so they helped to trigger the attack.

Custer immediately set the regiment in motion; at about noon the command passed over the divide toward the valley of the Little Bighorn. They were still some 15 miles from the huge Indian encampment, but they were moving at a fast trot. The encampment lay on the far side of the river, which ran between banks from five to ten feet high in places and offered few convenient fords. One of these fords was upstream, in the direction from which the cavalry was coming. One was near the center of the Indian camp, which was about three miles long. A third ford lay farther downstream, just below the camp.

Near the headwaters of Ash Creek (later to be called Reno Creek), which ran down to the river at the first ford, Custer stopped the regiment and divided his command. He assigned one entire company and details from each of the others to guard the slow-moving pack train. He assigned three companies of about 125 men to Benteen and told him to sweep the bluffs well south of the valley, scouring them thoroughly for Indians. After Benteen rode off, Custer assigned three more companies to Reno and ordered him to go directly down the creek, cross the river and charge upon the southern end of the camp. Custer, with a five-company main force of some 215 men, would support him. Reno supposed that Custer would be riding behind him, to follow up the initial collision with the great Indian community ahead. But instead of following Reno across the ford, Custer swung to the right, remaining on the other side of the river. Hidden behind high bluffs, he rode downstream, parallel to the Little Bighorn.

Custer's motives and intentions in fragmenting a force that in its entirety faced almost impossible odds have been discussed ever since, and many different explanations have been offered for his behavior. But the controlling facts of the drama that followed may have been rooted, very simply, in Custer's personality. Every victory he had ever won had come from plunging to the attack. He was a man of immense personal courage—he

had rather too much of that ingredient, General Sherman once observed—and he may not have felt those inner stirrings of mortality that warn other men of danger and doom. His confidence in himself, and by extension in his regiment, was boundless; when one of his men suggested that there were too many Indians ahead of them, Custer answered that there were not too many Indians on the North American continent for the 7th Cavalry to handle.

The only fear he felt, apparently, was that the Indians might yet flee to the south and elude him. Just before he ordered Reno to charge, a scout on a hillside saw a handful of Sioux running for the main camp and shouted, "Here are your Indians, running like devils." If the Indians were indeed in flight, his own horses were so worn that his troops could not catch them. These horses had not been watered since the day before; oats fell from their dry muzzles as men tried to feed them. And if the Indians vanished to the south, Custer's failure to obey Terry's instructions would become a crucial element in the final judgment of his conduct.

Clearly, Custer's mind was focused more on preventing the Indians' escape than on the strategy of fighting them. He sent Benteen ranging to the west to block them if they broke through. He sent Reno to charge them from the south in a diversionary attack that would have the effect of holding them in place. And he rode down to strike them in the heart.

With his command divided, the odds against his five-company force were overwhelming. Bouyer protested against the march into the valley and Custer accused him of cowardice. Bouyer shrugged and said, "If we go in there, we will never come out." Bloody Knife bade farewell to the sun in sign language, saying, "I shall not see you go down behind the hills tonight."

Reno rode on, joined by most of the scouts and their commander, Lieutenant Varnum. Only Bouyer and a few other scouts remained with Custer. Custer turned right, paused to water the horses at a small branch of Ash Creek, and went forward. At least twice he halted his men and rode up on the bluffs to peer across the river. For the first time, he could see the size of the Indian village—and he was elated. Because no effort was being made to strike the lodges, Custer apparently believed that he had caught the Indians napping. He waved his hat and yelled to his men, "We've got them this time!" From the bluffs he sent a sergeant hastening back to bring up the packs. The sergeant told the men in Benteen's column, which had begun to circle back to the regiment, "We've got 'em, boys."

The Custer column rode on. Just before turning into Medicine Tail Coulee, which led down to the river at the central ford, Custer sent back another message, this time to Benteen. Scrawled hastily by his adjutant, Lieutenant W. W. Cooke, it read: "Benteen. Come on. Big village—be quick—bring packs. W. W. Cooke P.S. bring pacs." The message reflected Custer's confidence: it was not Benteen's three companies of armed men he wanted so much as the packs with their ammunition. There was no suggestion of concern, either in the message or in the report of the messenger, Trumpeter Giovanni Martini. But Martini did say that at the top of the coulee he had looked back and seen Indians rising and firing from the brush on both sides of Custer's command. They had fired on him, too, wounding his horse as he galloped back toward Benteen. So the 200 men had ridden down to meet the thousands.

Reno had asked no questions when he was ordered to attack the southern end of the village. His total force amounted to about 134 officers and men and 16 scouts, but he assumed that Custer would be right behind him. When that assumption proved unfounded, his little charge began to come apart. Though he had made a good record in the Civil War, he had never before led a fight against Indians. So he was here on his own under strange and dangerous circumstances, and he did not perform well.

He took his three companies to the ford at a trot. The horses drank briefly, muzzles submerged in the cold water, and in about 15 minutes they were across the 25 to 30 feet of belly-deep water and re-forming on the other side. Then Reno launched his attack upon the village, some three miles away, galloping down the valley at a pace that was faster than some of his recruits ever had ridden a horse.

Warriors came out of the village afoot and on horseback to meet the threat from the south. They did not appear anxious to close, however; they wheeled about, raising a great cloud of dust, and as Reno neared they seemed to fall back toward the village so rapidly that he suspected a trap. Ahead Reno saw—or thought he saw

—a shallow ravine from which hundreds of warriors swarmed against him. Suddenly he ordered his men to halt and dismount. The order caught his men by surprise; up to that point there had been no actual fighting, though several hundred warriors were moving on the field before them. Cavalryman George F. Smith's horse ran away with him, carrying him straight into the Indians; he was undoubtedly knocked off his horse and killed in a moment. Then Reno ordered every fourth man to take four horses and retire to a stand of timber to the right near the river. The remaining men, about 80 in number, formed a thin skirmish line, its right end anchored in the timber. Each man stood about nine feet from the next and many, especially the recruits, were firing rapidly and wildly, though most of the Indians were still hundreds of yards away.

Thus Reno halted his attack. Technically, he had disobeyed the order to attack the village and some critics believed he had thus left his commander in the lurch. Others argued that if he had advanced he would have been cut to pieces within 500 yards. Wherever the truth lay, one fact was clear: in halting and dismounting Reno had shifted from offense to defense, and cavalry loses most of its effectiveness when it goes on the defensive. Furthermore, he had no hope of sustaining his position; the mounted Indians soon swept around the end of his line—in military terms, they turned his left flank—and had him in a deadly crossfire. His men began to bunch up, which made them better targets, and several were hit. As the Sioux turned his left flank, they also slipped up the river on his right flank, preparing to take his men and horses in the woods.

Reno began to order the men on the skirmish line to retreat to the woods, but soon some men who had received no orders at all began to yield to pressure. Most of the men stopped firing; immediately, the Sioux moved in close, and several more soldiers were hit. Defense was better in the woods, which were heavy with undergrowth, but finding a better defensive position did not help Reno to carry out his orders. He and his men were perhaps a thousand yards from the nearest lodge of the village; all chance for an attack was gone. The whole point of their being there was disappearing; already they were thinking in terms of sheer survival.

The Indians set fire to the dry river-bottom grass and buffalo-berry brush, and the flames worked into the thorny rose and plum-brush undergrowth, the cotton-woods and box elder. Warriors came in on their bellies under the smoke, rising, shooting, dropping out of sight. Arrows pricked the horses, and they reared and whinnied in pain; some lifted the men holding their reins off the ground, some jerked free and bolted. Several frightened soldiers were firing off rounds as fast as they could.

The position was serious but not yet desperate. Reno peered upriver, searching for Custer's promised support. It did not come, of course; Custer was miles away, across the river and heading for the village. As more and more Indians surrounded Reno's little force, he ordered a move to the bluffs on the far side of the river. A captain shouted, "Men, to your horses: the Indians are in our rear!" A scout turned to Reynolds and said, "What damn fool move is this?"

Many of the soldiers did not hear the order. They were still firing when the rumor ran among them, *we're getting out.* Uncertain, they looked around, searching for their officers, their friends, their horses—and of course they stopped firing. In the lull, a group of Sioux burst suddenly into a clearing and fired a point-blank volley from less than 30 feet. Reno was beside Bloody Knife, desperately querying him in sign language as to the Sioux intentions, when a Sioux bullet struck Bloody Knife between the eyes. It shattered his skull, and brains and blood flew across Reno's face.

That horrible moment apparently released the panic that had been rising in Reno. Though he and many soldiers were already mounted, he lost sight of his immediate plan, which was to leave the timber and bolt across the river. Shouting excitedly, his hat gone, he ordered the men to dismount, and as they began to do so, to remount. He himself swung back into his saddle and his horse leaped out of the timber in flight as if it had been spurred. The soldiers thundered after him.

The soldiers ran and they left their wounded, which meant certain death for the helpless men. There was panic, but it is not easy to condemn Reno, who was fighting odds of perhaps 10 to 1 and might not have saved any of his men if he had clung to that patch of timber. It is to his lasting discredit, however, that he abandoned his wounded and that as he led his men through a lashing crossfire he made no attempt to maintain order or cover his rear. In an orderly withdrawal, soldiers shoot as they move and keep the enemy busy. If they

run, the enemy can pick them off like animals in a hunt; in fact, as in a buffalo hunt, the Indians rode alongside the fleeing men and brought them down.

Reno galloped for more than a mile parallel to the river and away from the village, making for a high bluff on the far side. At the bank opposite that bluff the horses were forced to jump four or five feet into the river. As they struggled across, the Indians followed them, pulling soldiers from their horses and smashing their heads with clubs. On the far side there rose a sheer bank, some eight feet high, an incredible climb for a horse. Varnum's horse threw itself at the bank and heaved itself upward at an angle that nearly made Varnum slide over its rump, but many horses toppled backward into the water, crashing on men and horses below. The horses milled in the water below the bank, fighting the current, frantic with fear, rearing as the men hurled them at the awful bank.

Meanwhile, Indians were coming along the bluffs from downstream and shooting down at the soldiers as they emerged from the water. Lieutenant Benjamin Hodgson, Reno's adjutant, took a bullet that passed through his leg and killed his horse in the water. A trooper thrust a stirrup at Hodgson and pulled him to the bank; Hodgson was climbing up when a bullet from above killed him. As they left the timber, Hodgson had said to a friend, "What is this, a retreat?" "It looks most damnably like a rout," the other officer replied.

The fight in the timber and the flight across the river had cost Reno a third of his men. They straggled to the top of the highest bluff before the Indians could reach it, and lay there exhausted, demoralized, awaiting another onslaught. Charley Reynolds died on the way to the river crossing, trying to cover the retreating soldiers. His horse had been shot, and the heap of shells found beside his body showed that he had fought long and hard from behind the horse's body before he was killed. But the game had not been all the Indians'. One of the men shot an Indian off his horse and came up the bluff with a wet scalp swinging in his hand. And high on the bluff, at least temporarily safe, Reno had apparently formed his own view of what had happened. Told by a doctor that the men seemed demoralized by the rout, Reno snapped, "That was a cavalry charge, sir!"

His men stationed themselves to meet the next attack but now, except for a few snipers firing from a dis-

Little Horn River.
June 28 – 76.

My darling wife.

Genl Custer
15 fifteen officers, and over Three
hundred men have been killed.
we arrived in time to rescue what
was left who had taken to the
bluffs. I am all right and
so are all our battalion, The
Indians fled on our approac
They had the remnants of the 7th
Car. surrounded and would have
killed the whole party in a day
or two. The battle field is simply
horrible. Two hundred & four soldiers
and officers bodies in one place.
The whole valley for two miles is
dead horses + soldiers. We start
this p.m. for Big Horn River at
mouth of Little H. with 50 wounded
Send this to Mother. God bless you +
return save in safety – do not
be alarmed. We anticipate no
further fights. Your husband
Mrs C.F. Roe Willis Fort Smith Charley

A savage cartoon *(below)* of 1876 expressed the nation's shock and outrage about the Little Bighorn. Four of George Custer's relatives *(opposite)* rode with the 7th Cavalry and died in the debacle.

tance, the Indians were leaving, galloping swiftly downstream toward the center of the encampment. Some men could hear firing there. Custer's giving it to them, the soldiers told each other, grinning and pleased. And after half an hour, Reno saw Benteen's column approaching his position. He ran out and waved to the captain. "For God's sake, Benteen," he said, "halt your command and help me. I've lost half my men."

Soon after riding off at Custer's order, Benteen had decided he was on a fool's errand. He moved west as instructed and scoured the land for about an hour; then, seeing no Indians, he turned back and headed for the Little Bighorn, where he knew he would be needed. He was ahead of the pack train when he received Custer's written order to hasten forward with the packs. That order apparently made no sense to Benteen; if Custer's troops were going into a hard fight, they needed his men more than they needed him to herd pack animals. He went forward at a brisk trot. When he saw Reno he assumed that he had found the regiment, for he did not know that Custer had further divided his command after sending Benteen away. But Reno did not know where Custer was. He knew only that he

had not received the support Custer had seemed to promise and he believed that the Indians would soon overrun his position.

At this point, the two men bogged down in confusion and indecision. Custer's written order to Benteen had obviously come from on ahead, and both Reno and Benteen knew that a lively battle was going on there. Yet Benteen did not obey the order to join Custer swiftly, nor did either man follow the classic military dictum that, in the absence of orders, one marches toward the sound of firing. Reno refused to move at all, in fact, until the pack train arrived to resupply his men.

Finally a junior officer forced the matter. Captain Thomas Weir, who admired Custer as Benteen decidedly did not, set off downstream without authority. He and his company reached a high point — known afterward as Weir Point — from which he could look down on both the Indian encampment and the field to which Custer had gone. By this time the heavy firing had died down. Weir could see no sign of Custer's men — but he did see clouds of dust and warriors milling about in the distance. Meanwhile the remainder of the command moved forward in the direction of Weir Point. On reaching a vantage point Benteen, for the first time, began to realize the enormity of the situation. Across the river he said he saw at least 1,800 lodges. The air was full of dust and powder smoke, and the hills had an odd reddish-brown color. Later he learned that, like Custer's scouts on the Crow's Nest only 12 hours before, he had been looking at one of the greatest herds of Indian ponies ever assembled.

The Indians saw the soldiers on Weir Point and moved against them, gliding up the slopes and around the troops on both sides. Clearly, the position was untenable, and the men retreated back to their position on the bluff. More men were lost in the movement and still another wounded soldier was left to the Sioux. But once on the bluff again the soldiers were fairly secure and they held off the Indians for at least three hours of heavy fighting. When darkness came the shooting slackened; as usual, the Indians suspended operations for the night. All through that night, as they dug rough trenches with hatchets, knives, tin cups and even table forks, the exhausted soldiers saw great fires glowing in the village below. They could see figures dancing against the flames and hear the sounds of rapid-beating drums

BOSTON CUSTER, BROTHER

Sickly, 25-year-old Boston joined the expedition, partly for the benefit of outdoor life, as a civilian forage master.

CAPTAIN THOMAS CUSTER, BROTHER

Twice a Medal of Honor winner in the Civil War, Tom led Troop C at Little Bighorn and fell near his brother.

HENRY ARMSTRONG REED, NEPHEW

George Custer's favorite nephew, 18-year-old civilian Autie rode with the 7th Cavalry as his ill-fated uncle's guest.

LIEUTENANT JAMES CALHOUN, BROTHER-IN-LAW

Calhoun led the 7th's L Troop to its destruction. He died on a rise several hundred yards from Custer's final position.

and triumphant chants carried on the chill night air.

No one knows exactly what happened to Custer. The messenger Giovanni Martini was the last soldier to see him alive, and when Martini rode off with his message for Benteen he believed that all was well. Soldiers studied the evidence of the battlefield afterward, and over the years Indians gave their accounts—often conflicting ones—of what had happened that day. The accounts conflict for several reasons, the most important being that the Indians tended to see battle in purely individualistic terms. They had little or no command structure, no units and subunits with a chain of responsibility leading to particular commanders; and it was difficult for them to reconstruct what had happened in terms of overall battlefield movements. Each warrior recounted what he saw and did as an individual. And even then, many of them, fearing retribution, preferred not to talk about what had happened.

According to the most generally accepted theory, Custer led his command to Medicine Tail Coulee, where Martini saw him come under the initial attack. Custer's next move, then, would have been toward the central ford on the Little Bighorn. The Indian camp—huge beyond his wildest expectations, the very personification of Custer's luck—lay directly across the river. And there, most likely, the battle was joined.

There may have been a thousand warriors facing his 200 men in that area alone. The Indians came across the ford and swarmed up the broken gullies all around. Custer, of course, never cared about odds; perhaps he charged, despite the numbers. But numbers alone can turn the fiercest charge. In the midst of flying arrows and bullets, with blue powder smoke blowing until eyes burned, horses crashing into each other, squealing and falling, milling in a panic of their own—in the midst of all this, Custer's firing, shouting, cursing men surely knew that, whatever their commander thought, they were in trouble.

Some of Custer's command may have been turned back near the ford. There seems no possibility that they actually reached the river. Probably they were driven to their right on a course that led them to high, open ground farther downstream. It was the natural place to go. It is an elementary rule to seek the high ground in a fight, and cavalry needs open ground to use its mobility, its speed, the weight of its horses. Perhaps they could

rally, perhaps they could even counterattack, perhaps they could hold on until reinforcements arrived, perhaps—but the Indians were driving them.

What none of them could know was that Crazy Horse, one of the few great battle leaders among Indians, was in the camp they were attacking. Although Indians had no generals in the structured military sense, many of them followed Crazy Horse because the tactics he suggested almost always worked. It was Crazy Horse who had decoyed William Fetterman at Fort Phil Kearny 10 years before, and who had been mainly responsible for defeating Crook at the Rosebud on June 17. It was Crazy Horse who now played a leading role in the tactics that would destroy Custer.

Custer moved up to the high ground in good order, taking an offensive posture at the fore, and setting up a defensive posture at the rear. Then the Sioux chief Gall, leading the attack on Reno, heard the firing downstream and entered the battle. With hundreds of warriors, Gall galloped downstream away from the bluffs Reno's exhausted men had climbed. Crossing the center ford, these warriors hurled themselves against Custer's rear. Custer dismounted L Company, commanded by his brother-in-law, Lieutenant Calhoun, and I Company, commanded by Captain Myles Keogh, a laughing Irishman universally liked in the regiment. The men moved backward step by step, firing as they went, covering the rear.

But Crazy Horse, with hundreds of warriors, had gone down through the encampment on the other side of the Little Bighorn, and had crossed the river at the lower ford. Now he was moving to meet Custer head on, leading his stream of warriors up the very hill that Custer was climbing from the other side. The Indians topped the final rise, on a high point ahead of Custer's retreating forces, and crashed into Custer and the three forward companies like hammers. Again Custer rallied; now he grouped his men back to back for a final stand. In the rear, most of Gall's warriors had dismounted and crawled close to L Troop, picking the men off one by one—mostly with bows and arrows. A warrior thus armed could hug the ground and shoot without sound or smoke to reveal his position, and without showing himself at all. He would fire up into the air, the arrow arching high on its trajectory and falling to strike a soldier silently in the back with appalling effect. Many a

soldier died that way, and in death lay face down, an arrow rigid and upright in his back.

Coming closer, Gall's men finally took L Company by storm, with Indian bowmen and riflemen rising to fire a volley and mounted warriors leaping over their own men, then falling on the soldiers and killing them in moments. No soldiers broke; they held, fighting in place and dying in place, where their bodies later were found. And the Indians moved on I Company.

Up above, Custer organized his defense. He was clear-minded until the end, as was evident from the strong placement in which his men's bodies were later found. Their positions could not have been better. They fought hard but their carbines were fouling. The pieces heated, the soft copper shells expanded, the ejectors cut through the cartridge rims and left them in place. Then a man had to hunker down and work the cartridge out with his knife while bullets clipped the brush around him and arrows thudded into the ground. With the car-

tridge finally out he would slip in another and fire again, while all around him his friends were falling and the horses were screaming and the dust and smoke were so thick he could hardly see.

Men's eyes burned with sweat and smoke and fear, but they held their places, their pistols ready for the moment when there wasn't time left to dig out another shell from a fouled carbine. They were brave men, most of them, the Indians all knew that. A year later, Sitting Bull said, "I tell no lies about dead men. These men who came with the 'Long Hair' were as good men as ever fought." And Brave Wolf said, "It was hard fighting; very hard all the time. I have been in many hard fights, but I never saw such brave men."

Down below war flutes sounded, high, thin, cutting through the battle noise, and the Indians rolled over I Company as they had over L. Again, the majority of soldiers died in place, swinging their carbines as clubs, protecting the rear, emptying their pistols—except for

219

the last shot, which some saved for themselves. That is how their bodies were found. A sergeant caught a horse near the end and made a desperate half-mile ride through fire that could have killed a hundred men before a bullet brought him down, and afterward an Indian spoke of his courage. There was an officer in a buckskin shirt who also rode through unbelievable fire. Finally his horse fell and, agile as any Indian, he caught another and leaped into the saddle and rode about, rallying and holding his men. Then the Indians lost sight of him; he must have fallen at that point.

At last Crazy Horse, his warriors behind him like a tide, rode over Custer and all his men, cutting them down to the ground. The Indians came in a great cloud of dust that covered the ground and hid the killing, and when the dust settled the white soldiers were gone. A handful of white men were running downhill, desperate now and a few in panic, toward the cover of trees on the river's bank; the Indians galloped behind them and killed them. And then it was over. The soldiers were all dead, the ground suddenly quiet, and the Indians, as they said later, were surprised as men are when a tornado passes and leaves quiet behind its awful roar. Custer and one third of the 7th Cavalry had gone under in less than an hour, from the first shot to the last.

Next day the warriors renewed the siege of Benteen and Reno in hard fighting that lasted until about midafternoon. Then, unexpectedly, the Indians struck their camp. By sunset they were moving south in a force that reminded Benteen of a full cavalry division. Finally, on the 27th, General Terry's troops came up the river from the north. His men found the bodies, 197 by count, on the hill. Custer's was among them, naked but not scalped or mutilated. He had two clean wounds, in the heart and in the temple, either of which could have been fatal. The Indians themselves did not know who killed Custer or how or when he was killed, and no one knows today. They didn't even know until much later that Custer was there that day.

The battle of the Little Bighorn was the U.S. Army's most decisive defeat during the Indian wars, but it also sealed the final defeat of the Indians and destroyed whatever chances remained for men of good will to bridge the gaps that separated Indians and white men. After the death of Custer and his men the national mood hardened; in Washington and in the field,

government officials and military leaders addressed themselves to the task of crushing Indian resistance once and for all. Companies of cavalry were expanded from 64 to 100 men each, and new recruits hurried to join as "Custer Avengers." General Crook took to the field and drove his men to their limit (pages 110-111) as if to make up for his desultory campaigns of the spring. Nelson Miles dressed his men in buffalo coats and slashed across Sioux lands all winter and well into 1877. Other columns cut here and there, crashing into Indian camps from all sides. The Sioux ammunition was exhausted and no replacements were to be had. Their warriors were killed, their villages destroyed, their food supplies burned, their women and children left homeless in terrible cold. Though fighting flared periodically for 15 years more, there was never again a real war or even a battle on the scale of the Little Bighorn.

So Custer's death marked the end of an era. New railroad lines continued to thrust through the West, towns and cities mushroomed, and settlers filled the land. And as the country changed, the role of the frontier soldier changed, too, but as always, many of the hardest and most dangerous jobs were his.

Soldiers still lived in drafty barracks on tiny isolated posts, unwelcome in many towns and invariably frozen out of the town's pleasures by its prices. They still responded to Indian alarms, but now they also faced white desperadoes who struck isolated towns or stopped and robbed trains, then rode lathering horses into the deep reaches of the badlands that dot the West. The bright notes of "Boots and Saddles" still sang out on the posts and the soldiers still mounted and rode within the hour, a few days' rations of 'tack and bacon and coffee in his saddlebags, dust rising in clouds from his horse's hoofs, hoping that the water hole ahead held water, fearing that the turn ahead concealed a rifleman. For years, as the Old West slowly matured into the new, the soldier's life remained such that when he lounged in his barracks with his pipe, a banjo plinking, an accordion wheezing, he sang with heartfelt understanding the words of one of his favorite ballads:

> Oh the drums would roll, upon my soul,
> This is the style we'd go,
> Forty miles a day on beans and hay
> In the Regular Army O.

The post-mortem: was Custer betrayed?

Just what had gone wrong at Little Bighorn? That question reverberated through a nation wounded in its pride and its loss of a popular hero. In the months after the debacle, Custer idolaters, led by Frederick Whittaker, author of a flattering biography of the 7th Cavalry's flamboyant leader, began to demand a scapegoat. They were not long finding one.

In a published letter that went to Congress, Whittaker tried to blow up a retreat by one of Custer's officers into a full-scale betrayal: "Information from participants in the battle," he wrote, "is to the effect that gross cowardice was displayed by Major Marcus A. Reno." Stung by the charge, Reno asked for an Army court of inquiry. The court convened in Chicago on January 13, 1879.

The 26 days of hearings produced a mixture of recollections and opinions from 23 veterans of the battle. Estimates of the Indians' strength ranged from 1,800 to 9,000. Custer's stand was recalled as having lasted from two hours to less than 30 minutes. Two mule packers said Reno had been drunk on the battlefield. Reno denied it, saying his pint flask had lasted three days; he took the final drink, he said, upon seeing the "most disagreeable sight" of the mutilated dead on Custer's battlefield. One officer, Captain Edward Godfrey, said the major had displayed "nervous timidity." But no one established that he had seen any cowardice by Reno.

After testimony that filled 1,300 pages, the court exonerated Major Reno, but some civilian critics, notably Whittaker, branded the verdict a whitewash. Reno died ten years later, still haunted by the old accusations. And Americans never stopped being haunted by the notion that they had been cheated in the loss of a hero.

Three officers *(left)* of an Army court hear testimony on the possible cowardice at Little Bighorn of Custer's deputy, Marcus Reno.

Custer battles away in W. M. Cary's pioneer Little Bighorn scene.

222

The many last stands of George Custer

On July 19, 1876, only three weeks after the Battle of the Little Bighorn, a Manhattan newspaper ran the first depiction *(below)* of that military disaster. A woodcut by one W. M. Cary, it spotlighted Custer braced against the rump of a dead horse, about to be mowed down by Indians but bravely battling on. It became the prototype for a popular art form, the Custer's Last Stand picture, which glutted the country for the next few decades.

Largely because the only survivor from Custer's forces could not talk (it was a horse) and because most Indians would not talk, the pictures were usually inaccurate. For instance, in each version on this and the next six pages, Custer is incorrectly armed. In fact, as in the picture on pages 230-231, he was saberless and had two revolvers.

Dressed in a Civil War general's uniform, Custer fires at Indians charging from an Alpine backdrop.

This version resembles an Indian Austerlitz. Custer incorrectly wears a buckskin shirt, but his worried expression is no doubt correct.

The most famous *Last Fight*, this 1895 lithograph was sent to 150,000 saloons by the Anheuser-Busch brewery.

One of the most accurate reconstructions, Edgar Paxson's 1899 canvas was painted after 20 years' research.

90,91 –
torical S
Washing
Congres
partmen
ver Pub
The Na
ington,
Human
Tilden
Museur
Montar
lic Libr
Over D
except
partmer
—From
courtesy
—From
Library
of Ariz
seum C
lections
West P
Beeds
Cranda
York Pu
ert Cra
York P
— On
vogel: F
West by
Mrs. Sa
and Ar
ing Arr
The T
130, 13
Schrey
Americ
Mr. and
from T
Indian-
inal pai
tesy Th
Wester
Wester
rus Bra
Library
per's V
Wester
145 —
schneid